ANTHROPOLOGY AND SOCIAL CHANGE

LONDON SCHOOL OF ECONOMICS
MONOGRAPHS ON SOCIAL ANTHROPOLOGY

Managing Editor: Anthony Forge

LONDON SCHOOL OF ECONOMICS
MONOGRAPHS ON SOCIAL ANTHROPOLOGY
No. 38

ANTHROPOLOGY
AND
SOCIAL CHANGE

BY
LUCY MAIR

UNIVERSITY OF LONDON
THE ATHLONE PRESS
NEW YORK: HUMANITIES PRESS INC.
1969

Published by
THE ATHLONE PRESS
UNIVERSITY OF LONDON
at 2 Gower Street London WC1

Distributed by Constable & Co Ltd
10 *Orange Street London* WC2

Canada
Oxford University Press
Toronto

© *Lucy Mair,* 1969

485 19538 0

Printed in Great Britain by
WESTERN PRINTING SERVICES LTD
BRISTOL

ACKNOWLEDGEMENTS

I have to acknowledge permission to republish material from the editors of *Africa, World Affairs, Indonesië*, the *British Journal of Sociology, The Advancement of Science*, XIX, 1962 and XXI, 1964–5, *Comparative Studies in Society and History*, the *Transactions of the New York Academy of Sciences*, and *Cahiers D'Etudes Africaines*, II, No. 6, 1962 and IV, No. 15, 1964, and to the Institute of Race Relations; also to the Institut Solvay, Brussels, for permission to reproduce a paper given at a conference on Native Economy in Africa.

CONTENTS

Introduction

This book includes some essays that were earlier published with the title *Studies in Applied Anthropology*. The substitution of the phrase 'social change' for the label by which my teaching post at the London School of Economics was described is no accident, but rather an admission. Anyone who claims to apply a theoretical discipline is offering to do something with it. All I have ever been able to do is trace out the changes that European technical knowledge, particularly under colonial rule, has brought to the societies which at different times have been called primitive, backward, underdeveloped, developing, and are at the moment officially, it seems, known as less developed.

DO WE APPLY ANTHROPOLOGY?

Anthropologists have always had to claim that this kind of study is useful, because it is expensive, and they are in competition with other specialists who put forward similar claims, perhaps more convincingly. Useful to whom, for what? Are we offering to tell people what to do, or how to do it?

Or can it be that what we actually offer is really neither? We have in practice sometimes been allowed to impart something of what we know to people whose aim it is to promote social change in less developed countries. Englishmen training as colonial administrators used to learn a little anthropology, Frenchmen and Belgians rather more. In Britain today teachers, health education-ists, community development and other social welfare workers, sometimes even architects, are 'exposed' to social anthropology for shorter or longer periods. Once this would have meant ethno-graphy: descriptions of the traditional customs of the peoples among whom the men and women taking the course might be expected to find themselves. There are no longer any colonial administrators. The various specialists I have mentioned learn, if they listen and are given enough time, what are the implications of the changes they are seeking to produce, and what has been the general effect on societies of simple technology of the stream of changes to which each of them is making his contribution. But this is not applying anthropology; it is applying one or other specialist technique with a little background knowledge of the human reactions to be expected.

Rather more was claimed in the heyday of 'applied anthropology', when Malinowski was writing his articles in *Africa*, the organ of a new institution (then) which could be said in a sense to have been founded to promote the subject. The founders of the International African Institute did not think of it as a learned society, but as an organization which should seek knowledge as the basis of enlightened policies. In 1932 they published a research programme the object of which was defined as 'bringing about a better understanding of the factors of social cohesion in original African society, the ways in which these are being affected by the new influences, tendencies towards new groupings and the formation of new social bonds, and forms of co-operation between African societies and western civilization'. This knowledge, it was argued, would enable those in authority 'to foster the growth of a healthy, progressive, organized society', and would assist all those with practical aims in Africa 'in determining the right relations between the institutions of African Society and alien systems of government, education and religion, in preserving what is vital in the former and in eliminating unnecessary conflict between the latter and African tradition, custom and mentality'. The emphasis was on the integration of innovation into an existing framework, with the implication that tradition should be preserved wherever possible and the rate of change be not deliberately accelerated. This was a tenable attitude in a period of economic stagnation and an age when the indefinite continuance of colonial rule was taken for granted. There was room for argument about what innovations were necessary, and here professional anthropologists, with their greater tolerance of customs 'repugnant to humanity and natural justice', were more conservative than the men with practical aims whom their research was expected to assist. In these circumstances there could be no application of anthropology in any meaningful sense; anthropologists were asserting principles that the 'practical man' was committed to reject.

But the African Institute Fellows were pioneers in the kind of anthropology that is directed towards the study of change rather than the reconstruction of a hypothetical untouched society; and if applied anthropology is indeed the study of social change, they can be said to have introduced it.

What else is it or can it be? Ought we to speak of applied anthropology when what we mean is indicating the social context in which knowledge from some other field is to be applied? Very occasionally an anthropologist has the opportunity of saying 'what will happen if . . .'. An example is Elizabeth Colson's (1950) excellent discussion of the likely consequences of recognizing the right to make wills in a matrilineal society where men who had property – and their sons – were beginning to resent the right of sisters' sons to inherit. But there are not many such; and the government of Zambia still does not recognize wills.

So while I think the study of social change is inseparable from any anthropological work at the present time, I regret that 'Applied Anthropology' should have come to be thought of as an independent subject. There is little harm in making it an examination option – except when examiners demand that the questions set should *not* include any on social change. But it is dangerously misleading to let people think they can study 'applied anthropology' as a short cut to some kind of welfare activity without going through the grind of mastering the principles of social structure.

APPROACHES TO THE STUDY OF SOCIAL CHANGE

To any British anthropologist social change is structural change. We have not found it profitable to see the process in terms of the acceptance or rejection of cultural traits, nor yet of the differential adaptability of different social systems, an approach which has something in common with theories about factors favourable or otherwise to acculturation. American political scientists have sought to predict the type of political system likely to develop in different African states from the characteristics of traditional systems, an exercise that might be more fruitful if any of the new states discussed comprised only one traditional system. Apter (1961) has divided traditional systems into those with instrumental and those with consummatory values. The instrumental are what Max Weber would have called rational, and it seems that Apter postulates a normal evolution from the consummatory to the instrumental, which accompanies the establishment of strong

central power. But what was important on the threshold of
independence, according to his theory, was what stage a given
people had reached. From this one should be able to calculate
where to expect parliamentary government in a federal system,
where 'cabinet dictatorship', and so on. Alas, the recent history of
most African states has demonstrated that their first preoccupation
is not with details of constitutions.

If, however, discussion is limited to the narrower field of the
fate of traditional authority in a situation where all social relationships are rapidly changing, Apter's comparison of Buganda with
Ashanti could be more fruitful. But a French anthropologist,
Jacques Lombard (1967), who has relied largely on Apter's detailed
histories for information about chiefs in English-speaking territories, nevertheless rejects his interpretation of the events in terms
of the traditional value systems. To Lombard other factors are
equally or more important: in particular the question whether
the new leaders come from within or outside the traditional *élite*.
In Buganda, as in Northern Nigeria, they were members of it;
but in Buganda, as Apter himself recognizes, the ruling class was a
bureaucracy recruited on principles which owed nothing to
tradition. Lombard remarks too that the 'new men' in whose
hands the fate of the traditional authorities lay did not necessarily
come from the same ethnic group or from groups with similar
values, and their attitudes were formed by influences extraneous
to any African system, notably in the case of the Francophone
leaders who were brought together in Paris because of the French
idea of what the advance towards self-government should be.

British anthropologists would find the latter type of interpretation more congenial. It is perhaps our tradition of intensive fieldwork that leads us to see social change as the cumulative effect of
individual responses to new situations, where Herskovits saw
cultures rejecting alien instrusions and Apter sees value systems
endowing whole societies with rigidity or flexibility. We look
rather at the new opportunities that present themselves to
individuals, and ask what choice they make and why, and we tend
to find that it is the existing situation of the individual, not of the
society or the culture, that makes him choose one way or another;
and that all do not make the same choice.

As Malinowski's injunction to 'weigh, measure and count' has
been followed by fieldworkers with a mastery of statistical

techniques, we have been able quantitatively to document significant aspects of social change. This has been done sometimes by the use of records, as with changes in the rates of divorce or polygyny; occasionally by a 'replication study' such as that which Garbett (1960) made of five Shona villages, taking up an earlier analysis and showing that over ten years the rate of migration to labour centres had doubled without any corresponding change in the social structure as measured by the proportion of kinsmen of different kinds; or by the return of an anthropologist to the field he visited a generation earlier. Not many anthropologists have had, or sought, an opportunity to measure social change in this way, but Firth (1959) on his second visit to Tikopia was able to document social and economic change in detail by comparison with the data recorded on his first field trip.

In 1929 Tikopia had virtually no contact with the outside world apart from missionary activity. In 1948 the regular recruiting of labour for work on other islands had begun, and already by 1952 this had had marked consequences. Population had grown and resources diminished, even without the dramatic effects of hurricanes shortly before Firth's arrival. His tables document changes in the distribution of economic resources, in exchange rates for different commodities, in the area of land cultivated and type of crop, in the siting and naming of houses; and change – or rather continuity – in lineage structure.

When we seek to explain the direction of change, most of us make assumptions derived from 'naïve introspection': that most men aspire to some level of material wealth and comfort, that all care for the esteem of their fellows, that many compete for power or prestige. Men have interpreted their own actions and those of others in this way for as long as we have documents to testify to it, and in the practice of our other major principle, 'participant observation', we can learn what reasons our acquaintances give for the choices they make and what motives they ascribe to their neighbours. To psychologists this is no doubt an amateurish way of proceeding, but no other way is open to an anthropologist who has not also studied this other discipline; and while there is no reason why any individual should not combine the study of psychology with that of anthropology, as others have profitably combined economics or law, there is equally no obligation to make this everyone's supplementary subject. We have to do our best with the tools of our craft, extending our knowledge outside it in the direction in which we feel the most need. In this particular context a psychologist could no doubt teach us to refine our methods if he wished to, but I am not aware that any of them has made the offer.

Moreover, it sometimes seems that the contribution of psychologists in this field, with its emphasis on early conditioning, makes the explanation of change more difficult than it need be. Of course every society is maintained by pressures towards conformity, but fortunately these are not so all-pervading that they can only be resisted by creating the chaos that was described as preferable by Leach in the Reith Lectures for 1967. Curiously enough, it was an *obiter dictum* of the Reith Lecturer himself, to the effect that in a lineage system descent is fixed but marriage allows choice, that made me think of social change as primarily a matter of extending the range of options. Of course there is nothing original in this. Economists with their gaze fixed on the allocation of resources think of nothing else.

The theory of traditional 'patterns' which somehow determine the form of new institutions can be very misleading, and is so particularly when the leaders of new states seek to demonstrate that their ways of meeting unprecedented problems accord with traditional values. Democracy which does not permit opposition is, they argue, the African kind of democracy. Socialism is the right kind of organization for Africa because property traditionally belonged to descent groups, land nationalisation desirable because 'land always belonged to the chiefs'. These analogies may be pragmatically useful in securing popular consent to political decisions, but they can only obscure the real nature of contemporary problems.

The essays that I wrote during the period of transfer of power in Africa may seem to be concerned, like Apter's political predictions, with problems that history has swept under the carpet. If they are worth preserving, it is because they approach African questions not as matters peculiarly African but as matters essentially human. Of course anthropologists are largely concerned with the study of societies organised very differently from their own, but they fail in their duty if they do not recognize, and make it clear to the world, that the members of these societies are not a different kind of being from themselves. It is their first task to show that, whereas anyone's calculation of advantage must depend on the social norms which constrain him, people in any society make these calculations in an equally rational manner. If you understand the rules of the game you can see what people are likely to do. This is what Huckleberry Finn did when the horse was lost and, saying to himself 'If I were a horse, I'd ...', he went out and found it. The use of this phrase to epitomise the ethno-centric man who assumes that every rational person must *act* – not calculate – exactly as he does is a shocking measure of the illiteracy of contemporary anthropologists. Of my political essays the one that still retains significance is that on *Race, Tribe and Nation*, which I hope may do something to counter the view that 'tribalism' is not only a moral defect but a defect peculiar to Africa.

An aspect of social change that attracted some attention at the end of the Second World War was the efflorescence in the South Pacific of millenarian movements to which the name 'cargo cult' became attached. As an African specialist I might never have heard of them but for the accident that I spent twelve months with an organization which was training cadets for service with the military administration of New Guinea; and I might never have thought of attempting to compare them with other instances of millenarism if I had not been drafted into an LSE team committed to produce a series of papers on religion for a meeting of the Association of Social Anthropologists. It was innocently supposed in those days that a collection of papers by the members of a single department could be expected to have a common approach to the subject discussed.

Not much had been written on the subject at that time, but just about that time a number of people began to write independently about it, somehow under the influence of a *Zeitgeist* I suppose. In the colonial field it did seem that resentment against alien rule among populations which either did not understand political methods of organized resistance or were effectively debarred from these found expression in such movements; and the interest of students may have been stimulated by the revulsion against main-tenance of colonial rule that was so strongly felt in the immediate post-war period. The movements described by Balandier (1955) in the (then) French and Belgian Congo dated from long before the war, as did others in Uganda; the latter were not described in any detail until Welbourn wrote about them some years later.

Worsley (1957) sought to link all the movements in the Pacific by a Marxist explanation, but accounts of them were coming out in such numbers that even his diligence did not keep up with them all. More recently Lawrence (1964), Burridge (1960), and Schwartz (1962) have published detailed accounts of particular areas.

At the same time historians and others have been examining comparable phenomena in the past. Their interest has not always been the same as the anthropologists'. Cohn's illuminating *Pursuit of the Millenium* (1957) looks at mediaeval messianism as the forerunner of modern totalitarianism, but it also offers for anthropologists data on the social background of messianism which they could not have obtained from their own researches. From Germany we have a compendium of millenary beliefs from all continents with an interpretation by Mühlmann (1961) from the social psychologist's point of view. His remark that for a millenary prophet to be accepted there must be a predisposing psychological condition among his hearers parallels in an interesting way the reports from New Guinea of populations in a state of expectancy, waiting for a message, experiencing the trembling fits associated with the cargo movements at their height, or asking, as someone asked Firth, whether he had 'brought the things' – the phenomena that Firth (1955) has described as 'a cargo cult type of behaviour without a cargo cult'.

THEORETICAL QUESTIONS

Malinowski sent me to study social change because, he said, I didn't know enough anthropology for fieldwork of the standard type. Nobody today regards the study of social change as an occupation for the half-baked. But this is rather the status of applied anthropology. Students who have not been interested in generalisations about the nature of society, or have found these hard to grasp, are apt to be recommended by their teachers as 'better on the applied side'.

Nevertheless, if one is associated with the subject for long enough, theoretical interests keep breaking in, and I have included in this collection two essays which can hardly be said to have any practical application. That on clientship is another contribution to an ASA discussion, this time on social stratification. Again I was drafted and then found only one subject in my mind, which had come there, largely inspired by Jean Buxton's (1958) study of clientship in the tiny Mandari chiefdoms, when I was trying to picture how individuals in segmentary societies could build themselves up into chiefs. Clientship has also been discussed in West African political systems by Nadel (1942) and M. G. Smith (1960), and in more complex societies in Campbell's (1964) work on the Sarakatsani, Boissevain's (1966) on Sicily, and Bailey's (1963) on the organization of voting in Orissa.

The paper on witchcraft was prepared when I was asked to address anthropologists in Paris on recent work in this country, and does not purport to give anything more than a survey of current theory. Before this volume is published it will have been supplemented and corrected by the contributions to the ASA meeting in honour of Evans-Pritchard. This is a subject of perennial interest, constantly being reinforced by data from new areas such as that of Gelfand (1967) and Crawford (1967) on Rhodesia, and now beginning to profit from the interest of sociologically minded historians in classical and early European records.

I

Applied Anthropology and Development Policies[1]

In the last twenty or thirty years, gallons of ink have been spilt in discussion of the appropriate, or the inevitable, relation between scientific research and social needs, or, in more old-fashioned terms, between 'pure' and 'applied' science. At one extreme, 'pure' science is conceived as the disinterested pursuit of knowledge for its own sake. At the other, Marxist theory asserts that advances in scientific theory occur only in response to the demand for solutions to practical problems, though this does not exclude the value of 'fundamental' research, the bearing of which on practical problems is not immediately obvious to the layman. In the field which this discussion generally covers there is no doubt as to what is meant by applied science. It is the application of principles experimentally established to the production of specific results. In many cases the techniques based on these principles are so well developed that they can be practised by people with no more than an elementary understanding of the principles themselves, and indeed some of them are practised by all of us in everyday life. In others a scientist may be asked to solve a problem which falls in his field, but yet cannot be dealt with by the application of any principle already established; in these cases the functions of the pure and the applied scientist are combined.

Though some would claim to speak in an analogous way of the application of the principles of social anthropology, it must be admitted that the analogy is not a very close one. Indeed, in many quarters it is questioned whether anthropology is a science at all, and among anthropologists themselves there are some who hold that it is not and should not be. It is not, of course, an experimental science; it shares this disability with the other social sciences, apart from psychology, which can be studied experimentally to a

[1] Reprinted from *The British Journal of Sociology*, vol. 7, 1956.

limited extent. It can, however, claim to be something more than that study of the unique product of a particular series of events which Evans-Pritchard appears to have had in mind when he described anthropology as essentially akin to history. It does look for regularities in social behaviour extending beyond the limits of a single society, even if these must be of the 'natural history' type and not of the kind that the physicist can express in an equation. It has investigated the validity of theories of 'primitive communism', 'primitive pacifism' and a specifically 'primitive' type of mentality, and has rejected them in favour of interpretations which ascribe the special characteristics of the simpler societies, not to peculiarities in the nature of the people who compose them, but to the limitations of the techniques and resources at their disposal. This is a general proposition verified by observation, though in the nature of the case not by experiment, and it is of the first importance to anyone whose interest in the organisation of these societies arises from a desire to change it. It is the first step away from the assumption that any resistance to changes which the wise Westerner sees as desirable can be due only to laziness, stupidity, superstition or some other defect of character. The next, and indeed the heart of the matter, is the explanation of the complex of social pressures, of recognized claims and obligations, of values inculcated from childhood, within which every individual reacts to the attempts of strangers to improve his character, his way of life or his standard of living.

What anthropologists write when they are trying to interpret the African (as I shall call him for brevity, since I draw my own examples from Africa) to the 'practical man' is quite different from the kind of thing they write when they are analysing and comparing societies for the benefit of other anthropologists. But in the former case, are they acting like applied scientists, or even like the authors of text-books on applied science?

In one very important respect, they are not. Their books are not 'how to do it' manuals, providing formulae for the manipulation of society as the text-books of applied science do for the manipulation of matter. This is not to be explained simply by the relatively undeveloped state of anthropological theory. Indeed, an important achievement of anthropological analysis has been to show how much less easy it is to reshape society by deliberate action than has sometimes been supposed. The phrase 'social engineering', which some of us used with confidence a generation ago, is now out of favour.

The difference in the nature of the contribution that we can make towards the solution of practical problems is inherent in the nature of our subject-matter. That of the natural scientist is inert or without volition; in Africa he is asked to show how the swollen-shoot virus can be controlled, to find a profitable cash crop for an area of poor soils, or a reasonably cheap fertiliser, a prophylactic against malaria or a source of energy in a region with no coal. Attached to his solution is a large proviso which he is allowed to take for granted; his prescription will work *provided that people will use it.* Where it directly affects the mode of life of individuals, the people in question are the public in general; where it involves large-scale activities like the supply of power or irrigation, they are the controllers of the public purse. *As a scientist* he can work out the answer and say, 'Take it or leave it'; though if he happens to be by nature a politician, he will try to present it in palatable form. It is not, however, his professional research that tells him what is or is not palatable; his views on this subject will be drawn from incursions as an amateur into the social field. If, however, he fails to persuade, he has not failed in his task as a scientist; and he always has to face the possibility that a government may decide that what he recommends is too costly for the available resources.

The anthropologist's field of study is society. He cannot deal with a smaller unit than a number of persons linked by a network of socially recognized relationships, and his subject-matter is, not even the persons as organisms, but the completely immaterial relations – of claim and obligation, right and duty, superiority and subordination – that exist between them. If these can be manipulated, and some anthropologists do use the word, it must be in a very different sense from that in which iron ore is treated to make a steel girder or even malaria parasites killed in a human body.

They can, of course, be changed by external influences – directly by penalizing customary actions and imposing new obligations, indirectly by offering new opportunities. The civilizing mission of Europeans in the tropics, as it used to be called, the diffusion of technical assistance to underdeveloped areas, as it is called today, consists precisely in these processes. In the early period, the emphasis was on the whole more moral, in the latter it is more technological; though, at any rate in those territories for which the United Kingdom is responsible, we are as much interested today in making people democratic as our grandfathers were in making them Christian.

Some of the anthropologists who have given special attention to the social changes that these influences produce describe their work by the adjective 'applied'. The word recalls the confident 'social engineering' days in which it was born, and the fact that, historically, the founders of the International African Institute, the first body to sponsor studies of social change in Africa, expected the research which it promoted to bear fruit in enlightened policies. Predisposed to a sympathetic interpretation of African institutions and to those policies which sought to build on and develop these institutions rather than abruptly substitute others of European type, they expected that intensive field studies would provide governments with the data they were already looking for. To a large extent, they did so. They greatly increased the range of knowledge about the structure and operations of African political systems and about the nature of African civil law, notably in relation to land rights and marriage.

To administrators, however, the operative words have always been 'build' and 'develop', and it is here that the role of anthropologists becomes more difficult. Trained as they are to approach human institutions in an analytical spirit and to recognize how much all moral judgments are culturally conditioned, they do not necessarily share the administrators' assumptions as to what constitutes progress. On the other hand, they do not follow Westermarck's theory of ethical relativity to its logical conclusion of complete neutrality between different policies. When they have argued that the improvements which administrators have sought to make in the institutions of subject peoples were in fact no improvement, they have not taken their stand on the ground that there would be nothing to choose between the first state and the last, but have defended traditional institutions in terms of values shared by themselves and the administrators. Some have held the view that the colonial status is wrong in itself, and have argued that to integrate tribal political authorities in a colonial administrative system is a way of perpetuating this status and so deserves no assistance from them (cf. Firth 1938, pp. 195–7). Some have combined both attitudes. The second has something in common with that of the extreme pacifist who will not even succour the victims in a war. Granted that colonial policy has always taken into account, and often unduly, the interests of the imperial Power and its nationals, there is some room in every dependent territory, and a good deal in some, for action genuinely intended to further the interests of the inhabitants, and it is in this sphere that knowledge of their social organization is relevant. Some anthropologists, however, serve governments like that of the Union of South Africa, whose policies other anthropologists deplore; and this has been quoted as an instance of the use of scientific knowledge for anti-social ends (Nadel 1953, p. 9).

In the politically dependent territories, the refusal of anthropologists to buttress colonial rule has in fact had little part in its decline, and already the government of many of the tropical countries has passed to people who are alien only by culture and not by birth from the mass of their population. Of more significance have been the consequences of the development of anthropological studies themselves on the one hand and of policy on the other. The farther studies of African political institutions were pursued, the clearer it became that the 'Native Administrations' recognized by colonial governments had nothing but their personnel in common with their traditional predecessors, and in the sphere of civil law, though many people still sought to uphold traditional usage, as many were finding it to their interest to adopt the relationships characteristic of the modern commercial economy. The analysis of this process has been a valuable contribution to the study of society in general, but the conclusion to which it leads is that policies based on the preservation of traditional institutions, to which anthropological data were directly relevant, are now no longer practicable. Yet another conclusion which we cannot escape is that rapid technological change imposes a severe strain on small-scale societies. Its first result is a breakdown of traditional sanctions, and these are not easily replaced. Some American anthropologists go so far as to say that it produces a 'disturbance of basic personality'.

The older philosophy that was epitomised in the phrase 'Indirect Rule' has in fact been rejected. But in this development too anthropologists have had little part. It has been brought about mainly by the emergence of a western-educated class of political leaders in the dependent territories, who are committed to radical changes in both political and economic spheres, in a climate of world opinion sympathetic to their aspirations. Auxiliary influences have been those of the Western Powers, who, fearing that poverty may drive the tropical peoples to Communism, have a new motive for wishing to see their standards of living rise; of a considerable number of individuals who desire the same thing on purely humanitarian grounds; and of some technical authorities who have drawn attention to the dangerous destruction of natural resources by the farming methods of the tropical peasant. Faced with this last argument, the anthropologist cannot easily dismiss as 'materialistic' policies which must destroy the old social bonds; and indeed most of us, at times when the role of amateur doctor was forced upon us in the field, must have reflected that such medical services as were provided in the dependent territories were financed out of those very developments whose social consequences we had been deploring, and have felt that a good deal of social disturbance might be worth while if it raised the wretchedly low standard of health.

If it did. It is one thing to say that health cannot be improved without development, quite another that development is bound to improve health. The new rulers who believed that colonial exploitation was responsible for all their ills, the technical assistance teams who are offering their 'know-how' to the 'underdeveloped areas', are facing a problem that neither freedom nor technology can solve – how to induce the peasantry, in Furnivall's memorable phrase, to 'want what they need'.

Sometimes they turn to the anthropologist for the answer, particularly in America, where this kind of problem is new, and anthropologists have not yet lost the confidence that some of us in Britain once had. Why should not the anthropologist's 'how-to-do-it' manual complement those of the health visitor and agricultural extension worker? This brings us back to our starting-point – the content of the word 'it'.

The medical and the agricultural experts base their advice on 'prediction' in the simple sense that, in the field where their theories have been experimentally verified, they can say that what has happened before will happen again; certain biochemical processes will have certain consequences. Anthropologists – some of whom experience much heart-searching and sense of inferiority about the inability of their science to 'predict' – are being asked, in this context, not only to manipulate the immaterial, but to deal with situations the essence of which is that, in the anthropologist's field of inquiry, *they have not happened before*. In so far as the demand comes from outside and is not provoked by the anthropologists themselves, those who make it are either impelled by the naïve belief that there must be a technique for every problem, or think of 'natives' as having a specific 'mentality' the 'reactions' of which ought to be foreseeable by people who 'study natives'.

But the anthropologist's central problem is the nature of the forces that keep a society in being, that secure respect for accepted standards and some approximation to them of actual behaviour – in a word, the forces of conservatism. In so far as we can see regularities in human society, it is in the field of behaviour which is in accordance with these standards, and in the type of sanctions which secure uniformity. They are our nearest analogue, however distant, to the properties of material substances. Anthropologists who take a special interest in social change – and not all anthropologists do, for many think the study of established systems should be their primary task – inquire what are the circumstances in which new influences will be stronger than those making for conformity. But they too are aware that the mixture of rational calculation of advantage and culturally conditioned assumptions which maintains any social structure in being cannot be synthesised. It would be meaningless to ask an anthropologist to invent a new institution; it is the nature of the phenomena, not the inadequacy of his science, that makes this so. What he can do is to show where and why resistance is likely to be shown to innovations the merits of which may seem to their sponsors to be self-evident. This is not so insignificant an achievement that he need be ashamed of it. It is also sometimes possible for him, generalizing from the experience of other societies than the one under consideration, to foresee the implications of a proposed policy over a wider field than that which it directly envisages; this is 'prediction', as far as it goes.

The nearest approach to a 'how-to-do-it' manual comes from America, where Spicer (1952) has collected a number of instances where social factors blocked the introduction of technical improvements, presenting 'problem' and 'answer' separately so that students can try to work out their own solution. The solutions given consist for the most part in advice either on what to avoid or on what kinds of resistance to expect; a new cereal may give a better yield but not make such good pancakes, some other innovation may involve too difficult a re-organization of the labour force, a protest movement among mining labourers may have a social background very different from that which engendered the C.I.O. These are aids to analysis of the situation, and valuable aids; they are not prescriptions for action. The nearest approach to such a prescription is the advice to look for the group within which the sense of solidarity is strong enough to predispose its members to co-operate in new activities that can be shown to be in their interests.

Firth is the leading exponent in Britain of the view that the anthropologist's knowledge can be best utilized not in prescribing policies but in calling attention to the possibly unforeseen implications of the policies proposed by governments. To him this follows from the fact that the major premises of policy are predetermined, and that though the anthropologist may deny their validity he is not free to disregard them. I have suggested that it is in fact an inescapable result of the nature of our study; I shall have something to say later about the evaluation of policy by anthropologists. Firth illustrates his own principle in an excellent article (1951a, pp. 1–7) on the social implications of the Colombo Plan. In this he calls attention to the consequences of creating a middle class of technicians wholly dependent on their profession, if the speed of development is allowed to slacken so that many of these find themselves without employment. How to prevent this is clearly not a problem for an anthropologist; yet it takes a student of society to look beyond the simple assumption that 'development' will cure 'poverty' and so allay discontent, and foresee this situation. He also indicates the very radical change in the peasant's mode of life, and in the social relationships dependent on land rights, that are involved in proposals to substitute swamp cultivation for hill cultivation of rice; and insists that the advantages of such a change will have to be presented in very cogent form if they are to be accepted. Finally he explains some of the social attitudes that militate against that disposition to save and invest which, according to economists, is so necessary if people are to achieve the increase in productivity that will eventually raise their standard of living. Firth had also followed his own counsel that the anthropologist's function is to indicate the implications of alternative policies, and leave governments to choose between them, in a discussion of possible remedies for overpopulation in Tikopia (1936, ch. 12). Other examples of advice given in this form are rare.

These arguments are based on the results of general study of the peoples concerned, not on special inquiries made with the aim of 'applying' – that is, somehow utilizing – the data obtained. The term 'applied anthropology' has sometimes been used also of investigations in which anthropologists have collaborated with other specialists in fields where the latter hope to take action. Several such studies have been made on the subject of nutrition; in these dieticians have investigated the adequacy of the food consumed by some selected community while agricultural experts have studied techniques of cultivation and anthropologists the aspects of social organization relevant to the production, preparation and consumption of food. A study of a rather different type (unpublished) was recently made by Freedman in Indonesia, where in connection with a WHO campaign against kwashi-orkor, he looked for social factors with which the prevalence of the disease might be correlated and at the same time for explana-tions of the effectiveness or otherwise of nutrition propaganda. His specific recommendations are concerned with the organization and training of health workers; again, more 'What should they *know*?' than 'What should they *do*?' His own researches cover local attitudes towards food, health and medical practice; the validity of assumptions made in our own culture about the social factors leading to illness in children and of assumptions made by Indonesian doctors about the ideas and practices of their own patients; the type of propaganda which is understood; circum-stances such as the organization of household work or the low level of family income which may make it impracticable for people to follow the health educator's advice. In sum, it is a most valuable statement of the circumstances in which public health campaigns must operate. It also makes the point, which not only anthropologists have made before, that a campaign has little hope of success unless it enlists the support of influential persons in the community, and it gives the kind of information that anthropolo-gists are best qualified to give as to where such persons are likely to be found. This again is not a 'how-to-do-it' manual but rather a map of territory previously unexplored.

A valiant attempt to produce a theoretical principle which would be generally applicable in practice has been made by

Belshaw. He indeed seems to imply adherence to the view that no theoretical generalization which is not a guide to action has 'justification' (1954, p. 156). Writing with reference to development policies in colonial territories he argues that they consist essentially in altering 'the preference structure of a community'. But his actual prescriptions are not guides to action. One is that the balance of advantages of any policy against its cost should be calculated in terms of the values of the society concerned – a general principle, that of toleration or consideration of local wishes, which is not new, though it is seldom formulated in the language of the economist. The other is that 'ends', as he likes to call the aims of policy, to be accepted must be understood, and must not involve a conflict with social pressures inherent in the society which are too strong to be resisted. Since he believes that our science, now in its infancy, will advance to a much higher degree of precision in the future, he may hope that we shall one day produce formulae for detecting and measuring social pressures. But he does not even suggest any formula for directing them. So we again find that in practice the function of the anthropologist is to point to resistances inherent in social relationships, and also, of course, to 'growing points'. Why should he claim more? We are not specialists in public relations or in the art of persuasion.

Nadel also claims an important place for the anthropologist in practical affairs, and would sometimes seem to suggest, as Malinowski did, that the comprehensive scope of anthropology as the study of society as a whole should give his views priority over those of technical specialists in other fields. His own writings include examples of inquiries made at the request of governments, recommendations to governments, and forecasts of the consequences of existing trends arising from studies made without any practical aim. He has also asserted in general terms that, however inadequate the anthropologist's theories in comparison with those of the natural scientist, they nevertheless take him a good deal farther than the layman, and that if his advice is sought the blunders that he makes will at least be 'better blunders' (1951, p. 55).

When we examine the points on which Nadel has made practical recommendations, however, we find that for the most part they belong to fields in which those in authority wish to recognize existing institutions, and the main question asked is simply what these are. His study of the Nuba tribes of Kordofan was undertaken to provide the Sudan government with general information on their political system and civil law; it has some interesting remarks on the prerequisites for a successful federation for local government purposes (1947, pp. 492–3). When with the occupation forces in Eritrea he recorded the customary system of land rights (1945, pp. 1–22, 99–109); and in writing of the Nupe of the Northern Region of Nigeria he made an interesting estimate of the probable consequences of the introduction of mixed farming (1942, pp. 367–8). From a personal communication I learn that on one occasion during the war he successfully opposed the imposition of collective punishment on certain Somali tribes, on the ground that this was not in fact consistent with their customs and would not hit the persons at whom it was aimed. Each of these examples made a valuable addition to the information in the possession of a government. None of them, however, enters that contemporary field of policies aiming at extensive change which cannot be ignored if claims are made by anthropologists, or demands made on them, without reservation.

In opposition to the view I have suggested, that we deal with a subject-matter which is by its nature not susceptible of manipulation, both Belshaw and Nadel use the word, the former of something he thinks desirable, the latter of something that he considers dangerous. Belshaw appears to have in mind the secondary meaning of the word, that of 'using to one's advantage', since he describes policies in general as 'attempts to manipulate social processes'. Nadel, when he says the anthropologist can 'suggest how societies can be manipulated', implies something very sinister if this use of the word is intended. Possibly both writers are approaching the same subject from different points of view. Though it is unlikely that many men of affairs have much idea of what is meant by a social process, it is probable that, if they did, they might see more clearly the possibilities and limitations of political action and so frame their policies more intelligently; and this would be an element in that appreciation of the obstacles to be overcome which I have described as the anthropologist's most significant contribution to practical affairs. It is generally assumed that the policies in question are well-intentioned; and it is agreed that, if an anthropologist had reason to doubt this in a given case, he would be justified in refusing his co-operation. Nadel, however, considers that the 'manipulation of a society' might be for ends harmful to it, and that even if he refused to offer practical advice, an anthropologist might contribute to this simply by publishing facts. It is clear that this is a logical possibility; but before regarding it as a serious potential danger one would like to hear some examples of such hypothetical situations. It is in this context that Nadel quotes the Union of South Africa. He asks if the knowledge of anthropology is 'employed to buttress the obtaining policy and to strengthen the subjection of the native peoples' (1953, p. 9). To answer this question one would need to know not only more about the kind of information that is in fact collected by the ethnologists of the Department of Native Affairs, but also what kind of application is envisaged. Ethnographic data could perhaps be quoted to confirm the Nationalist view that Africans, as 'primitive' people, differ in something essential from Europeans; the burden of proving that they could be used in any other way to further the illiberal aspects of the *apartheid* policy, or to frustrate movements of opposition to it, would seem to lie with the maker of the suggestion. Nadel also refers to the use made by the United States government, in the late war, of anthropological studies of the 'character structure' of their enemies in planning 'psychological warfare'. Only an expert in this branch of anthropology could express a view on its effectiveness as a weapon of destruction.

Nevertheless, one cannot discuss the bearing of any branch of knowledge on practice without considering the responsibility of the scientist. Is this limited to increasing knowledge? Is it his right, or his duty, to demand a say in the activities for which his knowledge is used? Not many scientific discoveries have been as obviously double-edged as that of nuclear fission, which has so catastrophically become the *locus classicus* for this discussion. If the neutrality of anthropologists is not really likely to result in a disaster to humanity, or even to the peoples among whom they have worked, it may yet be that they do not wish to remain neutral, but would like to be regarded as specially qualified to say what colonial, or other, social policies ought to be. Also, they may be told that if they stop short of this they are not giving the full benefit of their knowledge to the world.

The social sciences occupy a different position from the natural sciences in this discussion, because ethical judgments are not external to their field of research but at the very centre of it. When social scientists present their results, they are describing human actions, on which their readers will pass judgment even if they themselves do not explicitly do so; and the way in which their description is worded will influence that judgment. The 'functional theory' in its extreme form held that the institutions of every society solved the problems of mastery of the environment through social co-operation in the way best suited to that society. Such a theory precludes any attempt to rank different societies in order of merit, but in order to make it convincing its adherents have to take every opportunity of defending institutions popularly regarded as 'barbarous' to a public that will not accept a defence based on the principle of toleration alone. Hence they are at once involved in appeals to the ethical assumptions of their public. Another theory is that, since all values are culturally determined, it is only our cultural conditioning that leads us to disapprove of any feature of an alien culture. Looked at without this subjective bias, all institutions are equally worthy of respect (or at least should be criticized only by people living under them). This theory has various weaknesses; it is inconsistent in that it makes a *Herrenvolk* attitude, which is a denial of itself, equally valid with one of 'cross-cultural' tolerance, and it has been pointed out that respect for alien cultures is itself an ethical principle.

It is obvious that anthropologists, who, like the rest of humanity, live as members of society, must recognize ethical principles in relation to their own actions, and it is unlikely that they will remain completely unmoved when confronted with actions among the peoples they study which run counter to the principles they cherish most.[1] Some have felt it a moral imperative to intervene to prevent homicide; such a necessity, fortunately, is rare. We have to try to practise a kind of emotional anaesthesia in the presence of values which may shock us, and to represent them as fairly as possible in our writings. In fact, however, most anthropologists have gone farther. Most of us have come to regard the peoples we have lived among as our friends, and have wished to give a sympathetic interpretation of them to readers who may include impatient emissaries of material, and indignant emissaries of moral, uplift. Our experience of people who follow different standards from our own need not lead us to the conclusion that

[1] This situation is admirably treated in fictional form in E. Smith-Bowen, 1954.

there is nothing to choose between different types of society, but it may lead us to a profitable examination of the question how far the rules of our own are rationally defensible.

If we abandon the principle of ethical neutrality, or, alternatively, find that we have never really held it, does this involve us in any practical consequences? Redfield, who in his Messenger Lectures has argued most persuasively against the principle, gives as one reason for rejecting it the fact that it is no use to an anthropologist who is consulted about a Point Four programme (1953, p. 145) – that is, of course, if the anthropologist is willing to help with the Point Four programme. This argument once more brings in what I suggest is the fallacy of supposing that the role of the anthropologist in the execution of these programmes ought to be a directing one. Anthropologists may have a higher status in the United States than they do in Britain, but my guess is that it will be only a matter of time before they learn by experience that their contribution must be limited in the way I have suggested by the nature of our subject. Though it doubtless depends upon individual temperament how much any anthropologist wishes to be employed as a consultant, I do not agree that to confine oneself to indicating the implications of policy is a cowardly shirking of issues, still less a refusal to put one's knowledge at the service of humanity. The question is sometimes discussed as if anthropologists were offered the opportunity of making recommendations over the whole field of policy, or at least invited to choose between alternatives. I am not aware that this has ever happened, but if it did, I cannot see that we could do otherwise, even if we had a definite preference for one, than make clear the social implications of both; that is, assuming that we are expected, like other advisers, to present a reasoned case. There remains the situation where an anthropologist may consider that some actual or proposed policy calls for a protest made in the light of his knowledge of its effects or implications. Anthropologists have not in fact imposed upon themselves any self-denying ordinance in the matter of protests. But when they protest, they must distinguish between their private moral code and their professional authority. We have no right to claim to be arbiters of morals, though of course we can argue that an actual or proposed policy is contrary to the moral principles to which its promoters subscribe; and, indeed, we need not expect to be listened to if we based a protest on any other grounds.

Though the makers of policy do not invite anthropologists to be their mentors, there are other sections of society where more is expected of us. It can happen that groups of people interested in promoting political principles seek the specialist assistance of social scientists, and ask from them not only information but programmes. They approach the subject, perhaps, with the expectation of the young H. G. Wells that the application of the appropriate sciences can remake the world; and when the hungry sheep are not fed with what they ask for, they are sometimes displeased and accuse the scientist of failing in his duty to society. But it is pertinent to ask whether the role of sheep is the appropriate one for them in this context. They do not choose their adviser for his sympathy with their aims, assuming, no doubt, that there is one right line which any expert in the subject would give. This is the moment to remember that anthropologists, so far from being ethically neutral, can be found to support quite different programmes. Though I have suggested that alarms about the use that might be made of the *data* supplied by government ethnologists in the Union of South Africa are exaggerated, there is little doubt that, if they were pressed to lay down general principles of *policy*, they would support those of *apartheid*. This might come as a shock to their audience, since in practice there is a certain association of the belief in the scientist as saviour with the belief that there are minimum human rights which the *apartheid* policy denies. But the logic of the position the sheep have taken up should lead them to accept it. Of course the sheep, who are not entirely imaginary, will not do so, but, idealists as they are, will turn on the shepherd as indignantly as they do on the anthropologist who does not undertake to lead them. In fact, at bottom they are not really sheep.

Nor should they be. They, too, like the policy-makers, have really chosen their ends in advance, and it is because it is their right and duty to do so that anthropologists should not claim to take over this decision from them. When Godfrey Wilson wrote that the anthropologist 'cannot, as a scientist, judge of good and evil . . . He can never either approve or condemn any policy as such' (1940), he was not putting up a smokescreen to cover retreat but refusing to be guilty of a monstrous arrogance. It is of some interest to note that the second sentence is followed almost immediately by a description of the social consequences of the labour policy of Northern Rhodesia that leaves the reader in no doubt whatever about his opinion of it. The greater the prestige accorded to the scientist, the more essential it is that both he and the public should distinguish what he can from what he cannot claim to *know*. There may be occasions on which, despairing of making his reasoning understood, he falls back on 'I'm not arguing with you. I'm telling you'; but he must not do this in fields where he could not argue from the data of his science. The nature of human welfare and, even more, the sometimes agonizing choice between the interests of different groups, or between incompatible ends which are both in themselves desirable, are matters lying within these fields.

The recent discussion in the press of the British Government's decision to prohibit the manufacture of heroin illustrates some of these points. Most of those who took part in it assumed that the prevention of pain was the end to be chosen, and argued the merits of heroin against other drugs. Some said the wrong experts had been consulted; specialists in medicine, yes, but in the wrong branches. A former League of Nations official, invoking another field of specialist knowledge, pointed out that measures other than forbidding manufacture had been found more effective against the drug traffic in the past. Some argued that any good that could be done in this direction would be outweighed by the suffering of patients who could not be treated with heroin (and would only benefit other nations anyway). Eventually five members of the Standing Medical Advisory Committee wrote a letter reaffirming the medical grounds of their advice, but adding that the choice between the social values in conflict 'cannot be made by the doctors alone but only by the Government'.[1] To this the angry rejoinder was made that 'we are told to leave it to Big Brother'.

This very succinct comment suggests, first of all, that the right of a doctor to complete freedom in prescribing treatment must be accepted as having priority over all other considerations; the analogy for an anthropologist might be a demand for priority at all times for a policy calculated to promote social stability, or satisfy national aspirations, or respect native values. It also suggests that, in leaving it to the makers of policy to resolve the conflict, we are treating them as repositories of superior knowledge. In fact we recognize their fallibility to the extent of requiring them

[1] *The Times*, 30 Nov. 1955.

to submit to the judgment of the general public at regular intervals, and this is not solely in order to allow groups whose material interests are opposed to compete for the control of policy. It is also because we all have, however dim, confused, inconsistent, self-interested, prejudiced, some idea of the difference between right and wrong action, and try to select to make the choice for us in cases as they arise people who we believe will decide in accordance with our ideas. Democracy may be easily deceived, as we are constantly reminded nowadays, but the remedy is not to surrender to someone claiming authority the control of that psychological process that old-fashioned people call conscience. We need more people, not fewer, to think about moral questions, and make up their own minds where the right course lies.

I do not suggest that they do this by some sort of innate moral faculty, and I do suggest, as I have said earlier in this essay, that they can be helped by knowledge of the different ways in which mankind has tried to solve the universal problems of living in society. Ginsberg points out that though moral judgments are 'ultimately traceable to primary experiences of value', they do rest on assumptions about facts, and it is for the social scientist to inquire into the validity of these assumptions. He remarks that to establish a rationally based moral system of general validity there is need for more 'inquiry into human needs and the laws of social interaction' (1954, p. 13). Here there is room for data from the simpler as well as the 'higher societies'.

Nadel suggests that certain criteria of evaluation are, as he puts it, 'entailed' in the concept of 'society' which is basic to social anthropology. 'Integration, regularity, stability, permanence are all requirements of society as we conceive of it: their disappearance means the dissolution of that very entity, society, and their strength or weakness a measure of social existence.' In addition, in the psychological field every culture allows gratifications and imposes frustrations, and the adequacy of any given culture may be assessed in terms of the relationship between the two. These two criteria may, of course, conflict, if, for example, social stability is maintained by 'the rigid exercise of force'; and in judging of such a situation we must, he admits, 'rely on our private convictions'. An anthropologist's training, however, leads him to think 'not only as a citizen or as a human being aware of ethical issues, but as one for whom citizenship and awareness of ethical issues are themselves problems challenging intellectual effort'. Despite all the difficulties which he recognizes, he asserts that the anthropologist's judgments on the worthiness of ends are more unassailable than those of others (1953, p. 16ff.). Those anthropologists who do not subscribe to dogmatic moral systems are certainly entitled to claim that they base such judgments on the rational interpretation of observed data, and those of their fellow-citizens who wish to reach their own conclusions in a rational manner can profit by the study of their arguments. But when the judgment itself is in question, if they ask him to make it for them they must remember that they are crediting him with wisdom as well as knowledge, and that wisdom is not a professional attainment.

2

Anthropology and the Underdeveloped Territories[1]

In these days every student of a specialized subject is liable to be challenged to demonstrate the value of his study. It is not enough to say that knowledge is good because it is knowledge. Different branches of knowledge are competing for students' time, and, even more anxiously, for money to pay for research. In the social sciences, where we concentrate on the various aspects of human behaviour, we scholars on our side are apt to think that if only people in authority would listen to us, they might take more intelligent decisions and make fewer mistakes.

In the presence of this audience there is no need to define the scope of social anthropology, nor to emphasize the aspects of policy to which knowledge of it is relevant. I think your great scholar, Dr Snouck Hurgronje, was ahead of anyone in the English-speaking world in realizing that the traditional customs of colonial peoples are not just a matter of antiquarian interest, that they do not simply vanish when confronted with what we call civilization, and that Europeans who are responsible for the government of these peoples must understand the rules and values by which they live.

It seems to have been only at the beginning of this century that American and English writers first urged that Governments should take anthropological knowledge into account. In America the occasion was the war with Spain, which resulted in America acquiring what any other nation would have called colonies. The American sociologist Keller published an article in the *Yale Review* in 1903, which seems oddly naïve when one reads it today. In his mind all the time is the simple notion of the survival

[1] Text of a lecture given to the Netherlands Africa Institute and the Royal Institute for the Indies at Amsterdam, 30 Oct. 1950, and reprinted from *Indonesië*, vol. 4, 1950–51.

of the fittest. Modern industrial civilization is clearly the fittest. In competition with its bearers, the indigenous inhabitants of various colonial areas have become extinct, or nearly so, and the rest must either adopt it or become extinct in their turn. But if we understand the indigenous cultures, we can make the process as painless as possible. 'Contending human races should be able to ease, at least, the extinction of their heavily handicapped antagonists.' That was Keller's view.

In Britain, anthropologists first tried to get a hearing in the South African War, after we had annexed the Transvaal and Orange Free State. They had had plenty of time to learn that the Bantu population there were not going to become extinct. In the context of the discussions of those days, they thought it necessary to point this out. They begged Mr Joseph Chamberlain to appoint a commission to study the customs and institutions of these populations before any legislation affecting them was passed. After many delays Mr Chamberlain replied that 'the officials of the new colonies are most fully occupied in the task of organizing the administration and in dealing with the numerous questions of pressing political importance which arise'. As a matter of fact, soon after the close of the war a commission was appointed to lay down principles of native policy, but it did not include any anthropologists.

Of course Keller took too simple a view when he thought the non-European peoples were doomed to extinction. But it does seem to be true that their cultures are fated to lose many of their most distinctive features. The colonial powers have brought their subjects within the orbit of western civilization. They have taught them to work for wages, and have taught some of them to read and write, and to aspire to professions that belong to the civilization of the western world. Today the indigenous peoples themselves want to adopt western civilization – or rather, some of them want some features of it. The conflicts and difficulties that we see among them today arise out of the fact that their adaptation is incomplete, and that fact itself is due to the contrast between their values and systems of obligation, their methods of social co-operation, and our own. We may not be as sure as Keller was that we know how to resolve these conflicts, but certainly there is only one person qualified to analyse them, and he is the anthropologist.

Anthropologists have always demanded a sympathetic hearing for the point of view of the peoples they study. One of the paradoxes of the colonial situation is that, apart from anthropologists and some administrators, most of the individuals who have direct dealings with indigenous peoples, and claim to 'know the native', see them through a mist of hostile prejudice – the irritation that arises out of misunderstanding, and the prejudice that every unthinking person has against people whose ways are different from his own. The modern anthropologist has to live in daily contact with the people he is studying, speak their language, and understand how they look on the new world that governments and employers have created. They become his friends, and unless he is an unusually diplomatic person, he often finds himself constrained to defend them against the kind of ill-informed criticism that he meets when he comes back to European circles. More important, his theory of society tells him that every society has its own inherent logic. It makes sense for the people who live in it. However barbarous its institutions may seem to Europeans, the native people can defend them – and not merely by saying, 'It is our custom'. The anthropologist can see objective reasons why practices that we condemn provide answers for the problems of the societies where we find them. They are crude answers, no doubt, but there are few indigenous institutions that could be dismissed as sheer barbarity or sheer stupidity, and simply destroyed, without leaving a gap that has to be filled. Because he knows this, the anthropologist is supposed to be a reactionary – a person who looks on the past as the ideal, who sees outmoded customs in a romantic light and stands in the way of progress. This criticism sometimes comes from the educated, nationalist, groups in the colonies, and sometimes from the anthropologist's own compatriots. At the present time most thinking people are convinced that there must be a very rapid adaptation in indigenous societies if they are to meet the problems of the modern world. This is as true of countries like Burma and Indonesia, which are now autonomous, as it is of territories still under colonial rule. I think there is actually no anthropologist who is not aware of this fact, though there are some who say it does not concern them – that they are interested in the simpler human societies simply as objects of study.

Why then should anthropologists, who claim to have

penetrated more deeply than others into colonial societies, and
who also claim to be the champions of the people whose lives we
study – why should we have misgivings about the changes
which are taking place among them? I think we could make a
number of answers.

One is that our analysis shows how complex the problems are.
We are not faced with a simple question of speeding up the rate
of change, but rather with what Godfrey Wilson, a brilliant
young British anthropologist who died during the war, called a
situation of 'uneven change'. Social change follows the line of
least resistance. People are readily induced to adopt new ways
by the prospect of immediate gain. They readily throw off old-
fashioned restraints if the new world offers them an escape from
such restraints. They are not so ready to accept new types of
obligation appropriate to the new types of economic relationship.

The layman interprets this situation in terms of the character of
the peoples concerned – they are lazy, they are dishonest, they
are self-seeking. The anthropologist knows that people's values
are not born in them but come to them from example and teaching
and experience, so he seeks the explanation elsewhere. To him the
society we should like to see is not just an agglomeration of
individuals who show the qualities of character that we like to
think belong to western civilization, but an integrated society.
By an integrated society he means one in which established
institutions, and the rights, obligations and values associated
with them, are generally accepted. To its members a society of
this kind is an intelligible world in which their place is clear.
The peasant societies of the tropical regions were of this type
before they were brought into the orbit of the world market.
Their material standards were very low, they had not the security
of life and limb that western rule gave them, the opportunities of
advancement open to individuals were limited, but they were
integrated wholes. Some anthropologists have attached so much
value to this fact that they have argued that it compensates for
all the limitations of life in such a society in comparison with our
own. Others, though they have not gone so far, have insisted
on the difficulties of re-organizing society in a period of rapid
change, and have urged that, in so far as western governments
can control the rate of change, they should do so, and should
at least not destroy indigenous institutions which still retain their

vitality. This was one of the arguments used in support of the British policy of Indirect Rule, and I think equally of the Dutch respect for indigenous authorities in Indonesia. Of course the policy itself did not depend on the advocacy of anthropologists. In so far as it was not imposed by necessity, it was the result of a spirit of tolerance which men like Lugard did not have to learn from anthropologists. Today the more popular view is that all indigenous institutions must disappear as soon as possible. The colonial peoples must transform themselves as soon as possible into modern states with all the institutions of the west. And if they are to have, and maintain, the independence that all are demanding and some have secured, they certainly must do this on the political side. In the British territories the most remarkable instance of such transformation that can be observed at the moment is the new constitution of the Gold Coast, which is to come into force in 1951. A Legislative Assembly is to be elected by universal suffrage, and from it will be formed an Executive Council whose members will have ministerial status. This council will differ from a Cabinet only in that it will be responsible to the Governor and not the Legislature. This will be a most interesting experiment.

The fact that British policy is now set on these lines has been quoted as an argument that anthropology is now obsolete, and that members of the colonial services no longer have anything to learn from its study. I think the situation is not so simple. In the first place, here is the most striking possible example of uneven change. A small number of educated persons are about to operate the political machinery of a modern state with an electorate consisting mainly of illiterate peasants, to whom the implications of an electoral system are entirely new, and the problems of central administration largely meaningless. I admit, of course, that all modern government is the activity of a minority of individuals aware of the issues among a more or less indifferent mass. But I would maintain that, in those countries of western civilization where the voter is allowed to exercise a choice, the gulf in experience and in values is not as wide as it is in the colonial and ex-colonial territories. And I would add that, in any case, studies of the type that anthropologists make, on the attitudes of the general public towards political issues, could be very informative in the so-called civilized countries.

In sociological terms the problem for the colonial peoples is a problem of re-integration. For today's generation the village and the tribe no longer enclose the world. The appeal of the market draws men outside. The opportunity of gain is followed rather than the path of duty, or rather, duty is forgotten when it hampers the pursuit of gain. We constantly hear of Africans who cannot advance themselves because if they are better off they are supposed to keep their poorer kinsmen, and these latter are invariably described as hangers-on or parasites. But there must be at least as many cases of old people past work who are neglected because the solidarity of the extended family is breaking down. We have not seen the development of any alternative to the obligations of kinship as a source of assistance to the needy, and we are not likely to as long as the small wealthy classes maintain their present aversion to taxation. Without going outside the bounds of African society, the organization of production is beginning to depend on wage-labour instead of family co-operation – excellent as long as there is some recognized standard regarding the respective obligations of employers and employed. But is there? In parts of Nigeria sons demand payment for working on their father's farms. The father's right to command has gone by the board. What will take its place?

Anthropology cannot give the answer to these questions. But it can claim a certain merit for having asked them. Apart from anthropologists, few persons associated with colonial territories, indigenous or immigrant, even know that they exist, though many are aware of anxieties or dissatisfactions the causes of which they have not analysed. The anthropologist is the expert with the requisite knowledge for making such an analysis.

Some anthropologists have claimed that they could not only find the causes of the dissatisfaction but remedy them. But the remedies they have offered have either been remedies which were already advocated on grounds of common sense or common humanity – such as securing to indigenous peoples land sufficient for their subsistence – or else they have consisted in urging that nothing should be done to make the maladjustment greater by destroying indigenous institutions. This is another reason why anthropologists are called reactionaries. As I have said, we see now that that answer is no answer. We cannot solve the problem of uneven change by trying to prevent change. We must seek to stimulate the necessary further changes that follow from the initial ones. The problem is, as Mr Furnivall has put it, how to make people want what they need.

Nobody at present has a very satisfactory answer to this problem. Colonial powers have tackled it at the material level by external pressure of various kinds. They all have their policies of village improvement in which they seek to induce the peasant to build better houses, to keep his village clean, to preserve the fertility of the soil, and so forth. They are all perturbed to find that persuasion works too slowly and compulsion leaves no lasting effect after it has been withdrawn. In England a year or two ago a conference of administrative officers from Africa was held which discussed for ten days the question how to stimulate initiative among Africans.

Africans have their own answer – 'Leave us to ourselves and give us an opportunity to use initiative; then you will find it is there.' But this only brings us to the crucial problem of finding the type of initiative which will be directed to the general good and not solely to the advancement of the cleverer or more fortunate individual. Mr Furnivall sees the answer to all these questions in the force of nationalism. He thinks that if nationalism is not just treated as subversive activity, but allowed to operate as a constructive force, it will inspire the indigenous peoples to the efforts which are needed to construct a new society. He points to the example of the rapid increase in literacy in Russia and China when those two countries decided that it was time for them to catch up to the level of the West.

It does seem clear that nationalism can give a very great impetus to the adaptation of indigenous institutions, and a much stronger one than can ever be given by a foreign ruler. But I cannot help wondering if the nationalist leaders themselves are not still impatient with the peasant's proverbial apathy and conservatism, and wondering how to overcome it. An anthropologist here would ask whether the problem is not the outcome of a conflict of values. The peasant farmer of the tropics is not lazy, as anyone who has watched him at work can testify. But in a subsistence economy, he cannot profitably do more than a certain amount of work, and so he learns to value leisure. When he awakens to the attractions of a cash income he does not cease to value leisure, and this makes it impossible for him to compete with those who value cash to the exclusion of leisure. Laziness is a relative term, with different meanings in different cultures. That is the anthropologist's analysis. It does not point to a course of action, but it does show, in one very simple example, why the habitual course, of upbraiding the peasant for laziness and preaching the virtues of hard work, is not effective. It suggests that it would be fruitful to investigate further the problem of incentives, to ask when and why does the peasant work hard as it is, what are his wants and ideals, to which of them can you appeal if you consider it necessary, in his own or the general interest, that he should work harder?

In general terms, I think I would say that the difference between the anthropologist's attitude towards these questions and the layman's is this. The layman supposes that for a colonial peasant community to develop into a modern state the separate individuals must develop the qualities that we think appropriate, and that we think we have – diligence, honesty, punctuality and so forth. The anthropologist's analysis shows that what is needed is the development of institutions, of appropriate systems of co-operation to which the appropriate values will be attached. But it also shows that to create the forms of these institutions is not enough. We can create them, but we cannot inform them with the values that we consider appropriate to them. The aims of the people who operate these institutions cannot be dictated. Here we have to leave it to the indigenous peoples to work out their own solution.

I mentioned that we are about to introduce a constitution based on universal suffrage in the Gold Coast. In Nigeria, elected local government bodies, with full constitutional responsibility for public services within their areas, are to come into operation next year. There is much speculation about how efficient they are likely to be. Will they balance their budgets? Will they take bribes, or insist on the employment of their own relatives, or steal from the funds? The anthropologist will ask rather different questions. He will look at them in their wider social context. What social classes are represented in them? Who are the people who make their will effective, and why? Do certain persons carry weight in virtue of their wealth, their family connections, or other relationships outside the council? Is there in fact any link between them and the people who will pay the taxes that they spend? Above all, are they going to be a means of associating the peasants with the management of their own affairs, or of consolidating an indigenous governing class?

I would not claim that, in relation to any aspect of colonial society, the anthropologist can do more than improve the analysis of developments by widening the range of the questions that are asked.

But there is one respect in which he can pronounce with certainty to the effect that existing policies, if they are continued, will make the emergence of a re-integrated society impossible. I would suggest that there are two pre-requisites for a satisfactory adaptation, and that in a considerable number of colonial territories these are absent. One is that those persons who have acquired modern skills and adopted modern values should be able to take their place as full members in the new commercial society, and the other is that the new economy should not involve the separation of men from their wives and children. As I said, in many places these conditions are not fulfilled. To take the second first, the reason is that agricultural production for the world market has rarely been based on the enterprise of individual peasants. Perhaps this would have been impossible in some cases. As a matter of historical fact, there are many where it was never tried. Estate production involves the concentration of a large labour force at a small number of points. Mines demand armies of thousands, and hundreds of thousands. The necessary population is never present at the outset in the near neighbourhood. If the situation had been met by the migration and re-settlement of whole populations, the social problem of developing in these new communities common standards which would be appropriate to an entirely new type of life would have been hard enough. In practice this solution was in any case impossible. If the new enterprises had had to wait for the spontaneous migration that built up the large industrial centres of the western world, they would never have become established at all. Indeed, they could not establish themselves without recourse to measures of force or fraud which the world today condemns, or at least without condoning such measures. This action was justified by the argument that in primitive society the whole burden of production is borne by the women, so that to make the men work for wages is to confer a benefit upon the whole community. The question of the ethics of compulsion in this form is no longer a live issue. Today the impersonal force of circumstances sends Africans on their journeys of hundreds of miles to the Rand gold mines or the Copper Belt, and we are now beginning to discuss the ethics of compulsory restriction on this movement. But many people still assume – or policy is framed as if they did – that the African man – and the South Sea Islander and the coolie in Oceania too – is a detachable part of the society to which he belongs, and can be removed or returned to his place according as European enterprise does or does not need him. This assumption is convenient for people who hold it, because it absolves them from many responsibilities that either the employer or the State must bear in a modern community – to provide family houses, pay a family wage, social services, insurance against those risks which either did not arise in the old subsistence society or were met by an appeal to the duties of kinsmen. If these things are not provided, it is impossible to build up an integrated society with the wage-labour of the able-bodied men as its economic basis.

But the pre-existing tribal societies are already in a state of disintegration, and the prime cause of this is the migration of the men to the centres of employment.

It is not only anthropologists who have noted this; as soon as any considerable proportion of the men begin to go away to work the results are apparent almost to the casual observer; on the economic side in houses falling down, ground not cleared for planting and consequent shortage of food, on the social, in deserted wives and children growing up without paternal control. Government agencies in most African colonies have counted the number of men away and know their proportion to the total manpower, and the figures themselves are regarded with alarm; in certain areas, anthropologists have examined the facts more closely and traced out in detail the effects on the societies concerned. Their studies reveal the profound internal contradictions of a society in which wage-labour is indispensable and which yet is not allowed to be a society of wage-labourers – a society whose accepted necessities include some which can only be bought for cash and others which can only be produced by direct labour, so that though work abroad is necessary, its product is not a substitute for work not done at home.

The most striking fact that these inquiries have shown is that under this system the economic requirements of the 'labour reservoir' societies cannot be met by the available man-power, since to meet them the same man would have to work simultaneously in places hundreds of miles apart. The younger men, working for their father's tax, their marriage payment, the equipment of a house, clothes for their children, now have the role which in Europe we call the bread-winner's – but bread is the one thing which they do not procure, and in their absence their families are short of food. Examination shows that the periods of absence of the wage-earners from their homes are growing longer and longer, their visits home not only more infrequent but of shorter duration. There is not, as might once have been hoped and is still in some quarters assumed, a rhythm of alternate work in the town and on the farm; there are long absences at work with short holidays at home. At the best, the absentees send money and goods home to their dependants; at the worse, they forget them and form new ties in the towns. In either case, the village in the tribal area is a place of women, children and old men.

The population of the towns is equally unable to become a coherent society. It consists predominantly of young men, either unmarried or with wives whom they have left at home. They do not stay long in one place, but travel to and from the rural areas and move from one town to another as they change employment. It is no longer assumed that they form the entire urban population. Most of the large cities now make some provision for family housing and also allocate land where Africans can build their own houses. A few mining companies provide quarters for their own employees. I think that on the Katanga mines there is a house for every African who actually has a wife. This is not the case in any British territory, and in relation to anything that has actually been found possible it seems a Utopian ideal.

Where living room is provided, it is hardly ever enough for a family with adolescent children or adult dependants. In these circumstances men hesitate to bring their wives to town and parents do not want to see their daughters go. Parents in the towns, if they have a sense of responsibility for their children, send them away to relatives in the country as soon as they are past infancy. It is almost impossible for old men past work to live in the towns, yet old people in the tribal areas may have no one to support them because all the members of the younger generation from whom they could claim it are away at work. Thus the traditional society of the native areas is being broken down, but there is no new community growing up outside. But if any social values are to be stabilized and preserved, they must be handed down from one generation to the next, and this is not possible if the generations are not in contact. In this system only a small minority of the younger generation maintain such contact with the elder. Again, for public opinion to be an effective social force there must be a group of adults in continuous contact; this condition is not present in the great majority of the urban populations. I say nothing of the poverty which forces Africans in the towns to means of livelihood that are contrary to the law. From the administrative point of view this is the major problem, and it adds disastrously to the difficulty of building up a coherent society with its own standards. But the root of the difficulty is the constant change, the lack of continuity, which is regarded with indifference where it is not deliberately engineered.

These are not esoteric mysteries. The facts are widely known and many people besides anthropologists are concerned about them. But I have tried to present them so as to show how the anthropologist interprets them from his point of view as a specialist.

We have to ask too whether he can be no more than an interpreter. I think the answer depends on two questions – whether he is able to recommend courses of action, and also whether the public in general believe that he is.

On the first point he is in the same difficulty as other social scientists. He is dealing with the sum total of the actions of whole populations, and that can only be controlled to a very limited extent. We sometimes think the 'practical man' makes the mistake of thinking that colonial populations are infinitely malleable, and warn him not to imagine that he can mould them exactly as he pleases. But if we imagine that, because we know these populations, we can claim to decide what policy ought to be, we are making just the same false assumption about our own compatriots. Popular prejudices and vested interests will not disappear at a word from us. Moreover, it is very rarely possible to offer a specific solution for a particular problem. The situations in which the problems arise are too complex. A pessimistic social scientist once went so far as to say that all that any social science can tell you is how not to make things worse. Certainly many of our researches have done more to reveal unsuspected difficulties than to make it easier for governments to attain their ends. We can often trace the disintegration of a peasant society, but we cannot prescribe the cure. We can only say what I have tried to say – that the prospects of recovery are more favourable in some places than they are in others. If we were to urge that the destructive forces should be restrained, that we should deliberately keep the traditional institutions in being for the sake of social integration, we should be silenced by the voices of the colonial peoples themselves. Among them the older generations regret the good old days, but the rest demand full membership of the modern world. Besides, change has gone too far for that remedy. The only way to remove the present maladjustments is by further adaptation.

The second condition is the attitude of the public towards us. Special knowledge cannot carry weight unless the lay public recognize its existence and wish to use it. Experts are called on to advise on malaria control because it is accepted that malaria is an evil and that the experts can deal with it; or on building roads and bridges because we are agreed on what we want in roads and bridges and we know who can give it us. But social integration is a commodity the general public have never heard of, though they may be aware of some of the consequences of social disintegration, such as the prevalence of crime. Yet this is the only subject on which we can claim to speak as experts. We may criticize colonial policies on general ethical grounds. Many of us do, and other people use the data we have collected to support this kind of criticism. But we are not experts on social justice. We are just unusually well informed laymen in that field. We have no right to claim that our view of social justice should be accepted *because* we are anthropologists.

What then is our contribution to the ends of colonial policy? Those in authority are apt to value information only so far as it helps them to attain ends they have already chosen. If they are told that their aims are unattainable, or contradictory, they dismiss such conclusions as 'impractical', and also the studies that lead to them. This consideration limits the field in which governments expressly ask the help of anthropologists. So we might have expected that at the present time, when the whole weight of Government support in Britain is given to the encouragement of westernization, our studies would be officially regarded as obsolete.

Fortunately this is not so. On the contrary, since the Colonial Development and Welfare Fund was created in 1940, the financial provision for research in anthropology in the British territories is better than ever before, and we do not have to depend on the generosity of American foundations, which used to be our principal source of support. Some of the investigations that this fund has made possible have been dictated by the personal interests of the workers, but others have been carried out at the request of governments who believe that they can utilize the results. Most of the major regions of the British colonial empire have been surveyed from the point of view of their needs in sociological research.

The type of work that is being done under these auspices concentrates on the process of change and its results. One field in which these consequences call for practical action is that of customary law – those systems of enforceable rights and obligations which all governments, however much they may have made rapid Europeanization their aim, have found themselves forced to recognize to a very large extent, since they reflect the relationships of daily life which are not changed by a stroke of the pen. Records of customary law may be obtained in various ways – by the comments of assessors on cases brought before European judges, for example, or by questioning selected informants. The special contribution of modern anthropological technique to this study is that it observes how the rules operate in practice, with all the evasions and compromises that are not mentioned when they are formulated in response to questions. Though there has seldom been much response to provisions intended to enable individual Africans to place themselves under the provisions of European law, abandoning those of their own custom, we are finding today that custom does not provide rules for all the situations that arise, notably in relation to commercial dealings. The gaps and uncertainties in the law administered by native tribunals today have engaged the attention of lawyers and could profitably be studied by anthropologists also.

In the special field of land tenure a number of studies are being made by anthropologists at the request of governments. The holding of land in a subsistence economy is so intimately bound up with the organization of groups for economic co-operation and so with the general social structure, that this is emphatically a subject on which the anthropologist's approach is important.

The type of work he would do in this connection may perhaps be taken as an example of the contribution which anthropologists believe they can make towards the understanding of colonial problems. They do not seek to recommend action so much as to lay a finger on maladjustments, to indicate trends, and to check the accuracy of current assumptions. In this case, how is the system of land rights changing in response to pressure on the land, to the introduction of ploughing, to commercial cultivation, to changes introduced perhaps as a result of other influences in the accepted principles of inheritance? Does it still give security to the cultivator in occupation? Is every man still able to claim somewhere the right to land for subsistence? Does this claim conflict with the aims of commercially-minded farmers who seek to establish unrestricted control over the land they have cultivated with cash crops? Is it a fact that a few individuals have secured large areas of land in a manner which renders others landless?

Another example of a recent study carried out at official request was an investigation of the social position of women in the British Cameroons, made with a view to finding out how education for girls could be best introduced. Anthropologists have taken part in nutrition surveys, in the studies of labour migration that I have mentioned, in some places they have compiled handbooks of native law. A number of social surveys have also been made which cover such points as changing family structure and marriage law, family budgets showing how the balance is changing between subsistence and cash economy, the structure and composition of newly-formed urban populations, emergence of new types of association, and so forth.

Not many of these studies produce proposals for specific action, and I would suggest that it is really a mistake to judge the ultimate value of the anthropologist's work by this criterion. In the long run, he can take his stand securely on the contention that every addition to our knowledge of the processes at work in colonial societies must be valuable. Its benefit is more likely to be felt as the indirect result of its gradual diffusion among persons having administrative responsibility, increasing their understanding of the situations with which they are dealing, than in direct recommendations on policy. In the conflict of values which is the central feature of colonial societies today, the anthropologist cannot claim to be the arbiter. The question, for example, whether a particular departure from customary behaviour is enterprise or exploitation is not capable of objective determination; it is determined in fact by a complex of competing interests and competing values, and no longer, in modern days, by paternal governments who can at least profess Olympian impartiality. It is better then that the anthropologist should be content to put his knowledge at the disposal of the framers of policy, leaving to them the responsibility for decisions into which other considerations must enter. He can fairly claim that governments would be unwise to disregard altogether the facts that he lays before them, and dismiss as 'reactionary' all those aspects of indigenous custom and social structure which present obstacles to the attainment of the ends they have chosen. Facts cannot be annihilated by ignoring them, and in the complexity of social change in the modern colonial world there is more, not less, need to know what they are than in the past.

3

Modern Developments in African Land Tenure[1]

African land tenure is a subject so vast that in dealing with it one hesitates to commit oneself to statements of general application lest particular instances should be found to controvert them. Yet, when it is considered from the point of view of culture change, it is possible to discern a number of general trends, the nature of which is similar because their cause is the same – the impact on African society of the commercial economy of Western Europe with its infinite range of forms of wealth and possibilities of acquiring them. Though other forces too are active in the modern process of culture change, this is the most pervasive, and its influence can be traced in the development of every institution. In the case of land rights, closely bound up as they are with systems of production, the influence is direct and obvious.

THE INDIGENOUS SYSTEMS

Certain very broad generalizations may also be hazarded concerning the indigenous systems of the agricultural peoples. In the first place, these systems were appropriate to a subsistence economy, where people obtained the goods they needed almost entirely by the work of their own hands, exploiting the resources of their immediate environment. In such an economy there could be no commodity more valuable than land, no circumstance in which it would be profitable to dispose of land. Land, in short, had no exchange value. Certain writers ascribe to African peoples an abstract theory of the sacredness of land which inhibits their recognition of its economic potentialities. Th. Heyse, for example, writes: 'It would be contrary to progress to seek to keep alive in the native mind the idea that the land is inalienable because it belongs to the living and dead in common' (1947, p. 17).

[1] Reprinted from *Africa*, vol. xviii, 1948.

The mythical charter, as Malinowski calls it, of rights in land, the conception of it as the home of the ancestor spirits, and the idea that to dispose of it is sacrilege (cf. Fortes 1945, p. 178), are indeed common features of African societies. Some of them also express in proverbial form the conception that the land must be preserved for coming generations. Yet there are not many recorded cases where someone who was invited to dispose of land for a profitable consideration has invoked such principles as a ground for refusal, though it is true that some of the chiefs who made the earliest agreements to alienate land were not fully aware what they were doing. When circumstances arise in which land can pass out of the hands of the group with a traditional claim to it, their reluctance to see this happen is formulated in terms of responsibility towards the dead or the unborn. Yet it would surely be unrealistic to conceive of these ideas as the primary reason why the right to alienate land is not commonly found in African custom; more fundamental is the absence of any motives for its exercise.

Secondly, two facts set limits to the amount of land which any individual would seek to utilize. Here the basic limitation was that imposed by technique; where the only implement known is the hoe, no one can clear much more ground than his neighbours. But, if he could, the second factor would come into play – that there was no incentive to cultivate more land than was necessary to provide an adequate food supply.

The level of technique also influenced the system of land rights in that, in the absence of any knowledge of manuring (and often even of livestock), the fertility of the soil could only be maintained by shifting cultivation; either the whole village was moved, or cultivation alternated with fallow in an area surrounding a group of permanent habitations. In the first case no permanent rights were acquired in any particular piece of land; in the second and more common, however, rights of occupation in an area large enough to allow for fallowing were normally acquired.

These then are the limitations set by circumstances to the development of African customary systems of land tenure. From the social point of view the essential common characteristic was that every individual had a right to the use of land derived, not from any economic transaction, but from his status either as a member of a kinship group or the subject of a political authority. The controlling authority of any settlement, whether a political chief or the head or elders of a kinship group, in the first instance allotted land to an applicant, whether a young man about to set up his household, or, in the case of a chief, any man who sought to attach himself to him. Once allotted, the land remained in his hands and passed to his heirs, and the original allocation was often large enough to maintain several generations of descendants. Thus sub-divisions of the settlement might be formed, looking to their own senior members as the relevant authorities for these units of land. The growing tendency of these sub-divisions to assert their independence of any wider authority is a feature of modern developments.

So long, however, as this wider authority was recognized, it had the right to reallocate land which was superfluous to the needs of any of its members. In addition, its consent was required for any transaction which conferred rights in the land of the group upon non-members of it. There were two principal ways in which this could be done. A man who was not using the whole area over which he had rights of cultivation might allot part of it to an outsider. The latter might be formally adopted into the group or ally himself with it by marriage, but if this was not done it was recognized that a member of the land-holding group would in case of need have a prior claim on the land. He was often expected to make a present at harvest-time to the right-holder on whose land he was living. Thus his position had points in common with that of a tenant, and the word is commonly used to describe such a person. But the essential difference between such an arrangement and the leasing of land as Europeans understand it was that it was not regarded by the right-holder as an economically profitable transaction. There was no question of turning to economic advantage land which he could not exploit directly or of calculation of payments in relation to economic potentialities; the advantage of the right-holder lay in the social prestige attaching to a man with dependants.[1]

The other way in which land rights could be transferred was by pledging land against a loan. Debts were most commonly incurred for the payment of fines or of bridewealth, or for the refund of bridewealth in case of divorce. Until the loan was repaid, the creditor was allowed to cultivate an agreed piece of land. Here again there was a fundamental difference from a

[1] Cf. *Report of the Committee on Native Land Tenures in Kikuyu Province*, 1933.

modern mortgage in that, after no matter how long a period, the land could be redeemed by the repayment of the debt.

These were the general characteristics of the system of land rights which the first Europeans found in Africa. To observers imbued with nineteenth-century ideas on 'the magic of property' their most striking feature appeared to be that the cultivator had in no case the absolute right to dispose as he pleased of his own land. Holding in addition the view that any form of government which was not a democracy must be a tyranny, such observers saw in the claims of African rulers to ultimate rights over the disposal of the land the justification of oppression against which the humble farmer must be defenceless, and pictured him in a state of constant insecurity, hardly able to count on reaping what he had sown. They did not realize that the features of the African system which appeared to them as defects would only be so in the context of a money economy, with the many opportunities that it offers of turning rights in land to profitable account. Hence what seems at first sight a paradox, but is, in fact, no more than a logical development: modern conditions have created in Africa the very insecurity which early critics regarded as inherent in the indigenous system.

In the period of subsistence economy, however, one might say that, although there was a degree of political insecurity, there was little economic insecurity. That is to say, anyone who was held by a powerful chief to have flouted his authority was liable to severe punishment, which might involve expulsion and confiscation of property, if not execution. Undoubtedly the result of this was to make life precarious for those in the immediate entourage of powerful chiefs. But there were limits set to such arbitrary action by the fact that every chief desired a large following, and that few were so secure from rivals that they could afford to make themselves generally hated. There was no question of depriving a cultivator of his land in order to turn it to greater profit. And where there was no powerful political authority this source of insecurity was not present at all.

NEW FACTORS IN THE SITUATION TODAY

Today the systems of land rights operate in different conditions. By far the most important new factor is the introduction of money, the acquisition of which opens up the possibility of an unlimited range of personal satisfactions. Land is no longer a unique commodity; it can be exchanged for money. Again, it is now profitable to cultivate land for other purposes than subsistence, and Africans everywhere are being actively encouraged to do so. From this two consequences follow.

In the first place nearly everyone is now cultivating more land, and since, at the same time, populations are increasing and soil fertility decreasing, and in some cases the available land has been limited by alienation policies, land has become a scarce commodity for which there is competition. In the second, there is competition for special types of land, of which cocoa farms in West Africa form the most conspicuous example.

In these circumstances the value of the consideration offered for the right to cultivate land will inevitably rise, and those who have the right to allocate it are not slow to turn this right to profitable account. The higher the value of the payment, the more anxious is the man who makes it to be secure in the rights which he has acquired; when his point of view is accepted and those granting the rights agree that they will assert no claims against him, the sale of land has begun, whether or not it is countenanced by the custodians of the law. In parts of West Africa the price of land sold outright is now twice the amount for which it could be pledged (Meek 1946, p. 159).

Complementary to the man who sees where money can be made from the exercise of rights over land is he who needs money and has no other way of raising it than by the surrender of land rights.

This is the man who, in the eyes of the early observers, was at so severe a disadvantage in that he had no secure title on which to raise capital for the improvement of his land. They sadly overrated the prudence of the husbandman, as they underrated the initiative of the moneylender. Though the heavy burden of debt that weighs upon the Gold Coast farmer has been incurred through the pledging of land or its produce, the sums that have been raised for productive purposes must be small indeed. A high proportion of the debt has been incurred in the attempt to keep up the standard of living that was adopted at the time when cocoa prices were at their maximum; of recent years it has been quite impossible for the majority of farmers to maintain this standard without borrowing.

An additional cause in this particular area is litigation over land claims, which has raged in the Gold Coast ever since gold prospectors began to offer payments to chiefs for the grant of concessions. As soon as it became apparent that there was money to be made in this way, neighbours began to assert claims over land on their boundaries in which they had previously taken no interest, and such claims were fought in one court after another till the costs amounted to far more than any profit that could have been derived from the land in dispute. They were met, first by contributions from the persons concerned, and later by pledging the land, so that it was lost through sheer anxiety to claim it as a source of profit.

Along with the changes in circumstances which make it worth while for the farmer to increase the extent of his cultivation have come other changes which make it practicable. He can use the plough instead of the hoe and thus clear more ground himself; or he can employ the labour of men who are also alive to the attractions of money but are not in a position to acquire it by growing cash crops. One consequence of this is the reluctance of individuals or subdivisions of a land-holding group to recognize the traditional right of the heads of the group to redistribute surplus land; it is perhaps the principal motive in the assertion by these smaller units of their independence of outside control. Another is a tendency for those persons who have authority to allocate land to take advantage of it, either to secure large areas for themselves or to allot them in return for payment – in the latter case, explicitly recognizing the transaction as a sale. Thirdly, rightholders find that their land may be made to yield more material satisfactions than the prestige derived from installing dependants upon it. Thus the position of the tenant today is really insecure; he may be evicted because the right-holder wants to plant wattle on the land where he grew his food crops, or even because he has planted it himself and the right-holder sees the way, by asserting his right of resumption, to secure to himself the resultant profit. The most striking instances of this type of development come from East Africa (See Phillips 1945, *passim*).

The types of development so far described are changes in modes of dealing with land which result from the exercise of existing rights to land in new ways in response to new incentives. They create, both for the African societies concerned and for the governments responsible for their administration, the problem of deciding which of these new ways is to be regarded as legitimate; in other words, what type of transaction the courts will uphold. One aspect of the problem arises from the desire of governments to influence the direction of culture change towards ends which they consider socially desirable – above all, to prevent the destructive utilization of land and its reckless alienation. Another comes from the fact that where land tenure is concerned, there is in every African society an opposition between those whose interests lie in the acceptance of new standards and those whose interests lie in the maintenance of the old. All kinds of cases occur where each side can put forward a claim that is entirely just in terms of the values which it accepts. Suppose pledged land is redeemed by an individual who has raised the redemption money by his unaided efforts. Should it return to the joint control of the group who pledged it, as custom would dictate? If the man who put up the money declares that he has no intention of surrendering control of land which, but for him, might never have been bought back, he has an argument which will command the sympathy of other commercially-minded Africans and of many Europeans.

Again, take the case of the tenant in a Kikuyu reserve. Most Europeans will agree with the old-fashioned African in condemning the sharp practice of the right-holder who evicts him to take his wattle plantation. But supposing the prior claim of the right-holding group is asserted in order to provide a holding for one of its members who has grown up in a squatter village in the settled area and decides to return to the reserve rather than enter into a labour tenancy, there may arise a conflict between two equally valid conceptions of justice. The youth has an admitted claim to a holding on the land of his kindred, but it is he now who is the stranger, compared with a tenant who may be farming the same land as his father and grandfather.

The solution will inevitably be found in the recognition of commercial transactions in land of the types known to European law, and measures to protect the weaker party – such as the recognition of a claim to compensation for unexhausted improvements – will doubtless be introduced on the advice of the governing authorities to temper the self-interest of the new business class. In parts of West Africa, however, a complicating factor exists which is independent of any of the forces described up to now.

This is the introduction of European legal forms in advance of the circumstances that have elsewhere given rise to commercial transactions. The trading companies who in the early days established themselves on the coast obtained the land they needed by agreements concluded on equal terms with the local chiefs, and drawn up according to the forms of English law. At a rather later stage, courts of law were set up to which native cases were brought, and these courts assumed that land could be seized in payment of debt. Then Africans began to qualify as lawyers and to introduce into dealings between their fellow Africans the type of document, purporting to confer the type of right, appropriate to transfers of land under English law. Today in the Gold Coast it is the rule rather than the exception for cocoa farmers to base their claims to land on documents, many of which have actually no legal validity.[1]

A conclusion on the process of culture change in general, applicable over a wider field than that of land tenure, is that with the introduction of a money economy any position of economic privilege tends to become a source of personal gain. Such privileges are the right to allot land and the right to claim labour or tribute in kind. In the closed economy of the past, the personal advantages to be derived from the exercise of such rights were limited and there was no temptation to the abuse of trust. Labour on the chief's fields produced a communal reserve of food and provided maintenance for the retinue which enabled him to carry out the tasks of government at the simple level of those days; tribute in kind served the same purpose. The chief could not use their entire yield for personal consumption, and their concentration in his hands was part of a process of circulation through the community; but as soon as they became convertible into cash the position changed. The substitution for these obligations in kind or in labour of payments to Native Administration treasuries is the answer given to part of the problem; but where the right to allot land, so fundamental an aspect of political authority in Africa, is concerned, the way to prevent abuse without destroying authority has not yet been found.

Another generalization of wide application is that the conservative force of tradition is never proof against the attraction of economic advantage, provided that the advantage is sufficient and

[1] Meek, *op. cit.*, p. 171.

is clearly recognized. In the case of land it is abundantly clear that the emotional and religious attitudes towards it which are inculcated by native tradition have not prevented the development of a commercial attitude. The classic case of African conservatism – the reluctance of the stock-owner to reduce the numbers of his stock and improve their quality – is also explained in terms of the emotional and religious attitude towards them that is so marked a feature of many African societies. But here too it may be that the emphasis should be laid on inadequate incentive rather than on conservatism as such. It is true also that the recognition of economic opportunity does not spread at the same rate to all the members of any society. In the case of land rights, changes designed to affect the mass of the population meet with as much resistance as destocking propaganda; the attempt to re-distribute oil-palm areas in Nigeria so as to increase the efficiency of cultivation is a case in point.

Some observers see as the essence of developments of the type described the emergence of the new system of values the acceptance of which is necessary if African productivity is to be increased and African standards of living raised. Others will regard them as instances of what the late Godfrey Wilson termed 'uneven change' (1945). It could certainly not be said that the stage at present reached represents a satisfactory adjustment to new conditions.

4

The Contribution of Social Anthropology to the Study of Changes in African Land Rights[1]

It has often been asserted that the absence of the conception of individual property in land is a retarding factor in the development of African agriculture. This proposition has more often been treated as an axiom than supported by arguments based on the observation of African systems in operation. I should like to examine its validity in the light of the studies that have been made by social anthropologists of (1) the actual nature of African systems of land rights and (2) the consequences which have followed the recognition or creation of individual property rights.

Of course I do not claim that all that I am going to say is esoteric knowledge which remained secret until social anthropologists penetrated its mysteries. Such a claim would be singularly inappropriate in this country, where Professor Guy Malengreau, whose special skill is, I think, that of a lawyer, has already most convincingly expounded several of the propositions that I am about to discuss.[2] I might, however, claim a certain common ground with him through the circumstances that the knowledge that we have of African institutions in the Congo has been very largely gathered by lawyers, who have done a part of the work that falls to anthropologists in British territories.

When Malinowski, at the time of the founding of the International African Institute in 1926, urged that the studies of anthropologists should be focused on those aspects of African society which were of significance for the framing of policy, he

---

[1] Paper read at a conference on changes in African land rights at the Institut Solvay, Brussels, Jan. 1956.

[2] Notably in his 'De l'accession des indigènes à la propriété foncière individuelle', *Zaire*, 1947, pp. 235–70, 399–434.

laid especial emphasis on systems of land rights as a subject of investigation. At that time African systems were widely misunderstood, and it is fair to say that the greater knowledge of their fundamental principles that we have today is due very largely to the stimulus given by him. Another British authority who has called attention to the importance of this question in Africa is Lord Hailey, who brought from his Indian experience the recognition that the type of land rights which are recognized or granted by the government can have a decisive influence on the development of an agricultural community. A panel of experts on land tenure convened at the Colonial Office in 1945, under his chairmanship, urged upon all African governments the need of a close study of the systems in operation in their territories and the changes which they were undergoing, as a basis for decisions as to the type of right which should now be recognized as valid. A good many such inquiries have been made, on lines which take the existing findings of social anthropology into account to a greater or lesser degree. But I should like to draw attention particularly to one or two intensive studies made by professional anthropologists.

The famous phrase of Arthur Young, 'the magic of property turns sand into gold', refers to a quite specific context – that of a system where individual property rights already exist, and are exercised by persons who hold them to the detriment of those who do not. It refers, in fact, to the insecurity of a tenant who has no protection against his landlord, and assumes an economy in which rights to the disposal of land are used as a source of commercial profit. There is no need to stress the fact that African traditional economies were not of this type. What then is the significance of the absence in African society of the conception of individual property in land?

The subject is sometimes discussed in terms of polar opposites – 'individual' and 'communal' or 'collective' rights – and the assumption is made that any system must belong to one or other category. Analysis of the data obtained by anthropologists suggests rather that within any African system there are two types of right, which may be called rights of occupation and rights of administration, and that the latter are held by different persons in different societies.

Certain principles will be found to be of general application:
(1) Every person has the right to land for cultivation in virtue of

his membership of some social group; (2) he has the right to remain in undisturbed occupation of this land and to transmit it to his heirs; (3) the group, or its representatives, have the right to veto any creation of rights in favour of non-members, and in certain cases to re-allocate land which has gone out of cultivation. Group rights come into being as a result of the principle that all a man's sons are his heirs; indeed, the land is often partitioned during the father's lifetime, as each son marries and a portion is allotted to his wife. Hence the group exercising joint rights is usually a group of kin. Sometimes, however, the overriding control is vested in a chief or headman whose authority extends over many others than his own kinsmen. In these cases the occupation of land depends upon political loyalty, and a landholder can be expelled as a punishment for disobedience. Here, and only here, can we speak of insecurity; and it is worth noting that it is not the insecurity of the tenant in relation to a landlord. The landlord, seeking to maximize his rent, readily exchanges one tenant for another. The chief seeks to maximize his following and does not readily drive away any subject; though we may agree that his decision that a subject is disloyal may sometimes be an arbitrary one.

If it is asserted that the absence of individual rights as we understand them is a deterrent to the adoption of commercial cultivation, we need only name a few crops that have been taken up with enthusiasm by African farmers who did not possess these rights – cocoa in West Africa, coffee in Tanganyika, wattles and maize in Kenya. In the Congo, too, as M. Malengreau points out, the areas under coffee, cotton and groundnuts are steadily increasing.

Deduction from the logical possibilities of a situation does not always lead to the right conclusion as to what will happen. In one or two cases the rules of customary tenure are incompatible with forms of land use which might be commercially profitable. Suppose that the arable lands are by custom thrown open after the harvest for common grazing, as is the case in Basutoland. As long as this rule is respected no one can plant a permanent crop. But the history of change in African land systems is precisely the history of the manipulation of the traditional rules in order to profit by new opportunities, and, sooner or later, the rejection of those that are found to be too irksome. It can rarely be demonstrated that any customary restriction on individual enterprise has prevented the introduction of a new form of land use which offered a good hope of profit. It is on record from Basutoland that one chief prevented the planting of wheat, and even destroyed standing crops, because the growers claimed the wheat straw as their own property and so the right of communal grazing after harvest was restricted. Yet it is taken for granted in Basutoland today that one of every man's three fields is planted with wheat (Ashton 1952, pp. 146 and 148). It is a matter for investigation how far the assertion often ascribed to African farmers, that they are afraid to have good fields because 'the chief will be jealous' or 'their neighbours will be jealous', is a genuine reason, and how far it is an excuse; and the same comment applies to the statement that people are afraid to excel their neighbours for fear of witchcraft. Witchcraft inspired by envy may be invoked as the explanation of some actual disaster, but it does not follow that anyone shuns prosperity in order to avoid the risk of witchcraft. It is significant that this kind of explanation of reluctance to improve methods of cultivation is most often heard in the regions where it has been hard to find a profitable crop. It is the answer to propaganda for soil conservation measures or for measures to improve the yield of the traditional food crops, from which the African farmer rarely expects to get benefits commensurate with the extra work involved.

In the process of manipulation of the traditional system in response to the opportunity of making profit from rights in land, the sphere of independent action by the small group or the individual right-holder is steadily increasing at the expense of that of control by the representatives of the wider collectivity. Although offers by governments to confer documentary title on anyone applying for it have rarely met with much response, persons who see the opportunity to dispose profitably of rights in land are eager to do so without appealing to any group authority. Commonly, too, the extent of the group whose members are willing to allow the re-allocation of surplus lands tends to grow narrower; as land becomes scarce, those in possession become more and more unwilling to relinquish control of fields which they may need for their sons, and if it has acquired a commercial value they want to enjoy the advantage from this. Developments among the Kikuyu, for example, illustrate this process. Of course it is logically possible that the problem of shortage could be solved by the insistence of those in authority on their right to redistribute the fields, and this is the solution we find in Basutoland. In this respect the Basuto seem to be peculiar. Why? Anthropologists have not sought to answer this question by comparative study, but I would suggest two reasons. The first is that among them land is not held by kin groups, but allocated to individuals by the political heads of districts, so that there is no close knot of kinsmen anxious to preserve the land for their descendants; and the second that, despite the scarcity of land, it has not acquired a commercial value sufficient to tempt the Basuto to make independent arrangements for the disposal of fields which are surplus to their needs or more than their man-power can plough. This latter reason must be associated with the fact that there is in any case a better income to be made from work outside Basutoland than from the produce of the land.

The farmer who has no security in Africa today is not the holder of land as member of a group, but he who has acquired his land by a cash transaction and does not know whether his claim is to be regarded as valid. Will the courts of the area hold that outright sale is not permitted under customary law? Will the sale be ruled invalid because all the members of the right-holding group were not consulted? Will the seller try to regain the land as soon as it has been planted up with cocoa or coffee, claiming that under customary law land pledged to an outsider can be redeemed at any time? It is for persons in this position, a position which has come into existence only in response to the new commercial opportunities, that there is need for individual title.

What happens in those cases where individual title has in fact been granted? There are a few cases in the African territories of the Commonwealth where the lands of a whole social unit have been parcelled out in holdings as individual property, held under European and not tribal law. The best known are the districts of the Transkei, in the Union of South Africa, which were surveyed under the Glen Grey Act of 1894, and the so-called *mailo* lands which were allotted in freehold to a thousand Ganda chiefs by the Uganda Agreement of 1900. Outside the Transkeian districts there are some villages in the Cape where land has been allotted to groups of Africans on individual title, or where it was actually purchased by the ancestors of the present inhabitants. In the Keiskammahoek District a sociological survey made a few years ago compared the present situation in villages where land was held on 'communal' and on individual tenure (Mills and Wilson 1952);

and for Buganda a study has recently been made by an African anthropologist, Mr A. B. Mukwaya (1953).

Since I took Arthur Young's saying for my opening text, I might introduce a summary of their observations by asking how the 'magic of property' has actually worked. Has either Keiskammahoek or Buganda been turned by it from sand into gold? Alas, we all know that in general the soil of Africa is changing in the opposite direction. I have suggested already that the incentive to demand the unrestricted control of land is the short-term profit to be made by disposing of it and not the long-term advantage of wise investment in it.

To the question, what does a tropical farmer do when given the full control of his land? the history of India has supplied an answer. He uses it as security for credit, but the money he raises is rarely invested in the land. This difficulty, and the dilemma that unless he can use his land in this way he cannot raise capital for productive purposes, are much debated. I know of no actual investigation by an anthropologist of such a situation, but I imagine that, if he were asked to comment upon it, he would look outside the narrow field of land rights at the whole system of values of the society. Is it necessary for a man to make displays on social and ceremonial occasions in order to gain esteem? Is it difficult for many men to attain the standard they aim at within the limits of their income? Do many of them really believe that long-term investment will in the end be worth while? Have they even ever been told that it will, in terms that they appreciate?

In the studies that I have mentioned, however, it is more interesting to see how far conceptions of the mutual obligations of kinsmen, and of other traditional social relationships, have modified a system of land rights which so many Europeans see as the key to African advancement, the way of escape from meaningless restrictions on the enterprise of an intelligent man.

The Keiskammahoek survey was carried out on lines first suggested by Malinowski; the history of a number of plots was traced out in detail, showing how they had been transmitted, subdivided and so on. When this method of study was first suggeated some thirty years ago, the comment was made that it would take 'an anthropological Methuselah' to complete the necessary inquiries. The value of properly selected samples, however, is now recognized, and in 1951 an article in the *Journal of*

African Administration, which is published by the U.K. Colonial Office for the information of officials serving in the African territories, recommended just this method to anyone proposing to make a land tenure survey.

In the village held under 'communal tenure', as the South African authorities call it, ten families were originally allotted holdings, but up to twenty years ago persons other than their descendants were sometimes given land. As is traditional with the south-eastern Bantu, the allocation of new fields was made by the headman. Now it is in practice the responsibility of the Native Commissioner, and the principles of customary tenure are being interpreted in a manner consistent with the aims of government policy. Of these the most important is that of providing land for cultivation to everyone who has a claim in virtue of village membership. This is in line with traditional principles, but now that land is scarce, it appears that another principle of the traditional system has greater weight with the African villagers, namely, the unbroken association of the holder and his heirs with any plot of land once allocated. In order not to lose this interest in his holding, a man who goes away to work will 'lend' it to a kinsman, and to prevent a field being transferred outside his family when he dies, a man may give one to his son during his lifetime. Thus we see again that individual interests assert themselves within the framework of a 'communal' system as soon as there is any competition for land. Men with no land, of course, invoke the 'communal' principle of redistribution.

Where land has been purchased, no control can be exercised over its disposal. In a village founded in this way, holdings had at one time been mortgaged or sold, but the practice had ceased as people became alive to the danger of losing their land.

It is often assumed that, once individual title has been granted, the land in question will continue to be the property of a single person. The history of Keiskammahoek shows that this is not the case. In fact, the holders behave as far as possible as they would if they had acquired their land in the traditional way by allocation from the chief or, as happens in other parts of Africa, simply by being the first to clear the bush. As long as there is surplus land available, the essentials of the process are the same.

Sometimes, when a holding is marked out, it is intentionally made larger than the area that one household can cultivate, on the

assumption that the surplus will be available for the next generation. If the original holding allows no surplus, or if there is no
demarcation of boundaries, then the ideal is for one son to remain
on his father's land while the others push out into the surrounding
bush. This process has been well described for the Kamba of Kenya
by Mr D. W. Penwill. The tradition he records is of a time when
the tribe were penetrating into new country and were ready to
abandon fields they had made for virgin land farther ahead; in
that case land already cleared would be handed over for some kind
of consideration, but a kinsman had the first right to acquire it.
In the freehold village at Keiskammahoek the only way of
expansion was to buy more land; but as long as the law allowed
this, all Africans who could did so, and the holding originally
purchased went to only one son of the buyer. But where this
expansion was not possible the land was divided among all the
sons, since it would be wrong for one to 'eat the inheritance alone'
and leave his brothers landless. Sometimes the lot is not divided
and so group rights come into being; sometimes boundaries are
formally marked out in the presence of all villagers. In either case
the principle which has priority is the claim of kinship. Eventually,
of course, the point is reached where further sub-division is
considered impracticable even by African standards; then some
men must become landless. In only one respect are the legal
implications of freehold acted upon. Since rights cannot be for-
feited by absence, some landowners live and work in urban areas,
and some of these lease their land for rent; if they have a kinsman
in the village, they will let him work the land without charge.

Thus, freehold gives security, but secure tenure does not lead to
the improvement of the land. 'Communal tenure' does not give
security, but this is because the right of administration is now in
the hands of a European whose ideas as to what constitutes a claim to
land are not those of African tradition. The Native Commissioner
recognizes the claims of close kinsmen to inherit land, but would
prefer to a distant kinsman, or a minor, some man who has been
long in the village without receiving an allotment. Thus the claim
to land as a member of a kin-group, the basis of the traditional
system, is no longer secure. In fact the extent of the group within
which re-allocation is allowed has been widened by European
action.

An obvious point on which I have not yet touched, which was

not obvious to Arthur Young, is that the units of land held by Africans under either of these systems are too small for any holder to derive an adequate income from farming alone. The confident assertion, 'Give a man the secure possession of a bleak rock and he will turn it into a garden', was conceived in the era when new technical discoveries seemed to offer unlimited hopes of improvement, and before agronomists had begun to wrestle with the difficulties of tropical soils and climates.

In Buganda the story is different. Here, as is well known, the Uganda Agreement allotted a total area of 8000 square miles in freehold to persons described as 'chiefs or private landowners', believed already to have the rights which freehold title would merely confirm. Here there was no question of holdings of uneconomic size. Since the number of persons entitled to freehold was estimated at a thousand, the average area of an estate should have been eight square miles. In fact the whole area was not allotted, and the number of claimants was nearly 4000, so that the grants actually made were of smaller areas. On the other hand, very much larger estates were allotted to the Kabaka, his close relatives and his principal chiefs.

Here one can certainly see how the landlords turned to profit the new rights with which they found themselves endowed. But it is even more interesting to observe the persistence of the traditional pattern of relationships between the holder of administrative rights and the cultivator of the land. The ways in which the system has developed have been analysed by Mr A. B. Mukwaya, on the basis of study of the central land register of Buganda and of the detailed history of 98 estates in two selected areas.

The total number of owners of freehold land has increased to a figure which Mr Mukwaya estimates at between 45,000 and 55,000. Hence the original grantees must have disposed of a good deal of their land. They did so in many ways. Some made gifts of portions to kinsmen or followers whom they wished to keep near them, but in many more cases a part of the original estate was sold. Indeed the sales of land began when the owners had to pay the fees for survey. Other sales have been made 'for such purposes as the purchase of motor-cars, the building of houses, or to raise capital to start shops or commercial companies and even to pay for luxurious living'.[1] Land is also sold to pay for the

[1] Op. cit., p. 35.

education of boys who then follow other callings than that of the farmer.

Why is it bought? Sometimes as a form of investment, but often because of the higher status accorded to the landowner as against the tenant. An essential of this status is that the landowner has his own tenants, who are subject to his authority in a relationship analogous to the traditional one between chief and subject. Hence not many men buy land to farm by their own or hired labour. The desire for security plays its part, but security is not sought in order to put capital into the land.

The claim of brothers to share an inheritance is still recognized in Buganda, but here group rights do not develop because the separate shares are demarcated, and because the unrestricted right of each heir to dispose of his land is recognized. In the cases recorded in detail the principal heir took by far the larger share of the original estate, but all the heirs gave away and sold portions of their land, with the result of creating a large number of small units (under 20 acres).

Indeed it is abundantly proven that the magic of property operates only in a very specific context, and no modern plans for the improvement of African agriculture rely on this principle alone. On the contrary, the greatest importance is now attached by some colonial governments to the retention of such control as may enable them to regulate farming methods. This itself is a source of difficulty in places where African farmers see that other Africans, or Europeans, have rights more extensive than they are themselves being offered; or where Africans trained in the principles of European law appeal to it as representing a system enjoyed by Europeans but denied by them to Africans. The political arguments for the grant of individual property rights may well be decisive in the end, but an anthropologist would suggest that they must be distinguished from attempts to advocate it as a contribution to the productivity of agriculture.

The Ganda landlords readily recognized the opportunity of deriving revenue from their tenants, the more so as the payments that they claimed were analogous with the tribute formerly due to the chief. The Uganda Government induced the African Government of Buganda to pass legislation fixing the sums to be paid by the tenant and protecting him from arbitrary eviction. The aims of this measure are beyond criticism. But one of its effects is that landlords who wish to lay out their land for mechanized cultivation are unable to find areas of suitable size on which there are no tenant holdings.

These facts abundantly demonstrate that proprietary rights in themselves have but little magical effect. Up to a point, they are not a prerequisite of development. M. Malengreau has argued that the traditional systems, in which rights in land depend directly upon cultivation, give a greater incentive to production than one in which a proprietor can leave his land undeveloped without losing his right to it. He points out that the direct incentive of a good price is sufficient to encourage the planting of cash crops. In fact there has rarely been any difficulty in inducing Africans to plant cash crops. The problem which concerns agronomists is the indifference of most Africans to those improvements in technique which are essential if the yield and quality of crops is to be increased or even maintained. This indifference is general; it cannot be said to be significantly greater in the case of those farmers who hold their land on some form of lease from right-holders, or who have bought it in an area where it is doubtful whether the sale will be regarded as valid. Nor can it be held to depend directly on the fact that land cannot be offered as security for credit. A social anthropologist would look for reasons in a wider field: in the whole range of traditional ideas about agriculture, in the tendency to find supernatural explanations for such misfortunes as the failure of crops, in experience of cases where the advice of the agricultural department proved unsound, in that preference for short-term, clearly envisaged benefits over more remote ones which is certainly not peculiar to Africans.

He would note that the actual work of cultivation is done mostly by women, who have far less contact with Europeans than do men, and are therefore least prepared to understand their exhortations and most disposed to regard these as mere tiresome interference by the authorities. He would also ask what is the constitution of the working team at the peak periods of farming activities. We know already that at these times no single household has enough man-power to complete these operations by itself. Many peoples have the system whereby all villagers work on each farm in turn, and are rewarded by beer at the end of the day. With others, every young man who is betrothed brings his age-mates to work on the field of his future father-in-law. Where cash incomes are high enough, wage-labour is employed. But until this point has been reached, the question what additional labour is needed, and where it can be found, is relevant to all recommendations for technical improvement.

In certain parts of Africa the anthropologist would observe a sense of insecurity that has quite a different source – the belief that Europeans are advocating the improvement of the land simply in order to take possession of it when the Africans have done the work, and, as the corollary of this fear and resentment, the conviction that there is no technical problem that the return of alienated lands to Africans would not solve.

The essential contribution of the social anthropologist to this subject is that he is trained to see any single change, of the kind that can be effected by legislation, against the background of an existing system of relationships and an existing standard of values. The new rules will be manipulated by the persons to whom they are applied in accordance with the views they hold of their own advantage. Some will seek to derive economic profit from the new situation, possibly in other ways than those the legislator hoped to encourage. Some will seek to realize old values, such as the close contiguity and co-operation of kinsfolk (which, as M. Malengreau points out, we praise when its consequences suit us), or the prestige of a landholding chief with followers grouped round him. What will happen in a given case depends on the relative strength of different social pressures and cannot be predicted in detail; but studies by social anthropologists have done a good deal to indicate the kind of development that may be expected.

5

Chieftainship in Modern Africa[1]

The contemporary development of African chieftainship is a question of considerable practical importance. The attitude which it will adopt towards the native chief in his relations with his own people is one of the major questions of policy which every colonial government has to decide. Some hold that a native society can only be satisfactorily ruled by – or through (the words are not quite synonymous) – its traditional head; others that the first duty of the civilizing power is to free its native subjects from the oppression and tyranny of their own rulers; others make it their aim to steer a middle course, and preserve the native authority in his traditional position while adapting his functions to the requirements of the present day. All have in fact considerably altered by their mere presence both the nature and the basis of the chief's authority.

Yet they have so far been content with a very incomplete knowledge of the political systems which they uphold or condemn. To the advocates of Indirect Rule, it is the sanctity of tradition that creates the claim to obedience, and for that reason the traditional chief is the ideal instrument for moulding native society in the form that civilization demands; to its opponents, authority in native societies consists in one-sided privileges maintained by the arbitrary use of force. Neither school of thought recognizes that such an institution as the chieftainship depends for its maintenance on a complex series of relationships which cannot be reduced to a single attribute. Thus, those who are for destroying it ignore altogether the question of the considerations of their own advantage which prompt the subjects to accede to the chief's claims upon them; while those who wish to preserve it are often in danger of overlooking the degree to which modern circumstances are changing its nature.

There are before us then two complementary questions – what

[1] Reprinted from *Africa*, vol. IX, 1936.

were the forces in native society which made the chief's power effective, and in what sphere did he exercise that power? That it consisted not only in exacting the performance of duties from his subjects, but also in rendering services to them, is, I would suggest, the key to a real understanding of this institution both in its normal working and in the distortion which it has undergone in modern times. I propose to develop this theory in connection with the chieftainship as it exists, and has existed, in Central and Southern Africa.

One might summarize the sources of the chief's authority by saying that it depended in part only on the supernatural sanctions attached to his heredity and in part on the due performance of his functions. By this I do not mean to suggest that any failure or abuse was instantly met by revolt and deposition, but rather that there was sufficient flexibility in the relations between governor and governed for discontent to make itself felt in ways which it was against the ruler's interest to disregard, while there were in practice often considerable checks on the abuse of an authority which was in theory absolute.

In the area with which I am concerned the functions of the chief might be of three kinds, magical, political, and economic, and his privileges can be closely correlated with the exercise of these functions. Everywhere the paramount chief or king is believed to stand in a special relationship to the land, and in virtue of this relationship he is frequently responsible for the performance of rites upon which the fertility of the land depends and which only he can satisfactorily carry out. It is especially in connection with these magical duties that his hereditary position, linking him as it does with the spirits of his predecessors, is of importance in validating his authority. Where the chief stands in this unique relationship to the supernatural powers which control the fortunes of his people, he might seem to hold all the trumps. Yet, in at least two tribes where this is the case, anthropological inquiry has found that in the political field his actions are circumscribed by the existence of councils of various kinds in which he does not hold a preponderant position, and whose authority is equal to his own.[1] Such facts emphasize the importance of looking for the source of political power not in the person of

---

[1] I refer to the Swazi and Bemba, who have been investigated by Dr P. J. Schoeman and Dr Audrey Richards respectively.

some individual who may seem to possess certain attributes of supremacy, but in the whole system which works to make authority effective in those spheres where authority is required.

The king's hereditary status is certainly an element in maintaining respect for his authority even where, as with the Ganda, he has no magical powers. Here his connection by descent with the mythological founder of the kingdom at the same time justified his claim to absolute ownership of the country and everything in it and guaranteed his adherence to the tradition which was formally reasserted at his accession – a tradition which, it is worth mentioning, laid down not only the supremacy of the king but his duty to respect certain rights of his subjects.

But tradition and mythology remain as ultimate rather than immediate sanctions for obedience to authority. It is not to them that we must look for the bases of the everyday acceptance of the chief's position and performance of the subjects' duties. That is to be found rather in the reciprocal nature of their relationship – in the interpretation of the subjects' duties as returns for benefits received. I do not mean to suggest that this was a conscious attitude, still less that tribute or labour were rendered out of spontaneous gratitude, but rather that the maintenance of political authority carried with it advantages to the governed sufficient to make them acquiesce in the burdens which it imposed upon them.

What were these advantages? They vary of course with the exact nature of the political organization in question. I can only speak in detail of the tribe which I know at first hand, the Ganda. With them the political functions of the chiefs, who formed a hierarchy appointed by the king and dependent for their position on his pleasure, consisted mainly in the administration of justice and the organization of warfare. I have myself heard an old peasant say that God showed the Ganda especial favour in giving them chiefs to settle their quarrels. Warfare with them went beyond the mere organization of defence, in itself a service of some importance, to constitute, in the form of raids on neighbouring tribes, a speedier way of increasing their material possessions than any more conventionally economic activity.

In economic matters authority might seem at first sight to have carried with it a position of pure privilege. In the first place, the subject's right to occupy land, and hence his entire livelihood, depended theoretically on the king and practically on the chief to whose village he attached himself. For failure to render the customary services, as for any other action displeasing to the chief, he was liable to eviction. Those who see in African chieftainship nothing but arbitrary tyranny may seem to find here an argument for their point of view, but for an analysis of the working of the institution what is relevant is that the services rendered by the peasant are not given in a one-sided submission to supernatural power or physical force, but in return for rights of fundamental importance. To the Ganda there was no injustice in the fact that these rights were not unconditional. Moreover, he had a ready means of expressing dissatisfaction with his chief by moving to another village, and since the chief's economic privileges gave him a motive for desiring to attract and retain a large following, this right was an effective check on tyrannous behaviour. At the same time, the chief's rights of eviction and of physical punishment certainly were an element in securing the obedience of his followers.

The rights which a chief could claim from his subjects consisted of a gourd of beer in every brew, a considerable portion of the goods paid over in compensation for any offence tried by him, and services when required in the building of his houses and the fence which surrounded them. He received also his share of the taxes collected through his agency at the command of the king, and on the return from a raiding expedition it rested with him to distribute among his followers that portion of the spoil captured by them which was left when the king had selected his share and, of course, to retain as much of it as he thought fit.

But this system did not mean a constantly increasing accumulation of wealth in the hands of the privileged few, for the simple reason that in the native economy satiation point was reached early, and when it was reached the rich man turned from the enjoyment of possession to the enjoyment of munificence. Generosity was expected of a chief and was the best way to increase his following; and on the size of his following depended wealth, prestige, and promotion to the control of a wider area. Among other peoples the accumulation of wealth in the chief's hands has been found to serve even more obvious social needs in an even more direct and obvious way, for example in forming a reserve against famine or providing for the maintenance of a standing army.

This very summary account of the relations between chief and people in Ganda society indicates the mutual dependence which formed the basis of the native political organization. To the peasant the chief was the ultimate source of his livelihood and a more immediate source of material benefits; he also represented the authority and leadership necessary for orderly relations in peace and the successful organization of war. To the chief his followers brought wealth and prestige provided he dealt fairly with them – a proviso which shows how the institution contained within itself checks on the abuse of a privileged position.

A further check existed in the system of succession. The hereditary principle did not mean that certain individuals were destined by birth alone to succeed to authority. There was always a certain range of choice, which made it worth while for persons who lusted for power to show themselves fit for it. Any son of the king might be selected to succeed him; while in the case of a chief the choice was even wider, extending to the sons of his brothers. Moreover, under the Ganda system in which chiefs could be transferred by the king from one district to another, a chief's heir did not necessarily succeed to the dead man's position. If this was important, a more experienced man might be appointed to it while the young heir was given a smaller village until his merit was tried.

A feature of the Ganda system which again limited the action both of the king and the chiefs was the existence, side by side with the theoretically supreme authority, of a counsellor whose influence carried very great weight. While the heir could dismiss his father's counsellor, he was not normally expected to do so; so that the new holder of any political position, from the king downwards, usually entered upon his office subject to the advice of an older and more experienced man. This counsellor's advice was asked before any drastic step was taken, such as the deposition of a chief by the king or the eviction of a peasant by the chief; and in the case of the chiefs he was the recognized channel through which peasants who considered that they were unfairly treated could express their grievances.

In describing this system I have not been guided by any sentimental desire to idealize a vanished past. I do not mean to present it as incapable of improvement or to suggest that the principles of government which European powers have set

themselves to introduce have no advantages. Clearly it left room
for many acts of oppression against individual subjects and gave
to the rulers a wider scope for the indulgence of personal feelings
and desires than Europeans in theory approve. I have been careful
to say, not that the system prevented the abuse of power, but that
it set limits to such abuse. Can we say more of the political
institutions of the most advanced civilizations? They have their
abuses, too, which seem less flagrant perhaps only because they
are more familiar. The main aim of my analysis, however, has
been to try to give a more complete picture than that usually
painted of a native system of government in operation, and by
doing so to indicate the kind of phenomena which ought to be
taken into account by those who set out to modify such systems,
particularly if their aim is to utilize them as part of an organization
on European lines. Indirect Rule has been defined as the progressive
adaptation of native institutions to modern conditions; but I have
suggested already that many administrations which purport to
have adopted Indirect Rule have not looked beyond one single
factor in the native institutions concerned, namely the hereditary
principle. Some have supposed that by merely preserving the
hereditary principle they have fully respected all native rights;
others have believed that provided they employ for the purpose
an hereditary authority they can induce natives to obey any
orders, however burdensome or unwelcome, that the European
government may decide to issue.

This rather superficial conception of the nature of chieftainship
has resulted in a general failure to recognize that the entire basis of
the chief's position has been altered by the very advent of European government. What was in many areas one of the most
important functions of the supreme authority has been completely
removed. I mean the organization of war, which in some African
societies has justified a system of government much more auto-
cratic than that which I have described among the Ganda. Even
where he has retained his judicial authority the modern chief
has lost the right to inflict severe punishments for offences against
himself. Where new systems of land tenure have been introduced
the fundamental economic relationship between chief and people
is broken. Christianity and the obsolescence of public ritual have
affected this relationship on the religious side. On the other side,
authority rests now, not on popularity or on the rendering of

specific services to the governed, but on the power of the European government, which, though it may remove chiefs from office, seldom does so for the reasons which would cause native opinion to desire such a step. It is for this reason – because it has put the chief out of reach of the sanctions with which he had formerly to reckon – that a government which maintains his authority without understanding its real nature may well be condoning abuses of it which could not in the past have been committed with impunity. Moreover, modern economic conditions create the possibility of abuses which could not in the past have been committed at all. The possibilities of turning one's economic privileges to direct personal advantage are now unlimited; yet the most superficially literal conception of Indirect Rule involves the maintenance of the chief's traditional privileges. Because they had dissociated these privileges from the corresponding responsibilities, those in authority have sometimes failed to see that under modern conditions tribute paid to chiefs is coming to be just that one-sided burden that it was sometimes thought to have been before. Yet these same conditions make any effective protest out of the question.

This is one way in which the nature of the chief's position as one part of a reciprocal relationship has been misunderstood. The possibilities of the other party – his subjects as a body, or any one of them – retaliating for his failure to do his due part have been removed; for it is only those who reject government through the chief altogether and propose to replace it by democracy on European lines, who have concerned themselves with the subjects' point of view, and they only misinterpret it by forgetting again that the subject had rights as well as duties. By removing the checks on the chief's action at the same time that they converted his payment in kind into a money payment, European administrations have shown that in the long run traditional sentiments and ethical standards do not prevail where the ruler has a clear interest in disregarding them, and perhaps that such standards do not even appear to be applicable in a situation so new as that created by the presence of the European trader on the one hand, and on the other by the accumulation in the chief's possession, not of cattle, maize-cobs, beer, or garments, but of that currency with which European goods can be obtained.

At the same time that they have altered the basis of the chief's authority in a way which tips the balance of power in his favour, even though he may no longer be able to assert himself by the use of physical violence, European governments have assigned to him many duties which did not form part of his functions before.[1] Some of these, such as the collection of census figures, enforcement of regulations for the destruction of old cotton plants, encouragement of such activities as the killing of rats, might be described as neutral in their effect on the relation between chief and subject. But others, those which involve the use of the chief's authority in calling upon his subjects to enter upon distasteful and arduous pursuits which bring them no apparent advantage and throw out of gear the whole routine of their lives, inevitably produce a complete distortion of that relationship. I refer, of course, to the use of the chief in obtaining labour for European employers, or recruits in those colonies where conscription is in force, in collecting taxes imposed by the government, and sometimes in enforcing the cultivation by natives of commercial crops. Where these are among the duties of the chief, he is simply an instrument of the superior government and is plainly recognized by the natives as such. It may be true that his prestige and generally dominant position gain him an obedience which an agent sent from outside would not obtain without resort to actual force, but it is quite mistaken to interpret this as meaning that the hereditary status of the chief justifies his every action in his subjects' eyes, and to conclude that in order to satisfy European interests without disintegrating native society, it is sufficient to make the chief their mouthpiece. The natives may continue to obey, but the chieftainship ceases to be a native institution, and they are as well aware of that fact as any anthropologist.

This last interpretation of Indirect Rule is one which would never be accepted by the original exponent of a theory whose basic principle is that the development of native society must not be subservient to the demands of the European market. But it contains elements that are also present in the popular attitude towards Indirect Rule sincerely conceived as the best vehicle for such a development. Here again it is argued that civilization can be made acceptable if it is introduced through the chief, and again the argument is only a half-truth. It is true that the prestige

[1] This situation is admirably described by Professor N. De Cleene in his article 'Les Chefs indigènes au Mayombe', *Africa*, 8, no. 1, p. 70.

of the chief often leads his subjects to imitate him in following European ways. Christianity itself has sometimes been adopted in this manner, not always without sudden mass conversion from one sect to another. But for the chief's example to be effective, the innovation must be in something which is either a matter of indifference to the people or else appears to offer them some positive advantage. And further, the apparent advantages may not always be consistent with the effective working of the complex of native institutions taken as a whole. It is just as easy for progress to become synonymous with disruption if an hereditary chief is made its apostle as it is where the native who claims to have become civilized is encouraged to reject the chief's authority – though the process of distruption may be less obvious.

I am not meaning to suggest that Indirect Rule is a chimera, that in modern conditions the chieftainship has gone through such changes that it is no longer recognizable as an African institution at all and might as well give place to something more efficient and more consonant with modern theories of government. On the contrary, I hold that the future of African society depends upon the success with which continuity and its attendant stability can be maintained in the process of transition which it is now passing through. My argument is that the link which unites the chief with his ancestors is not by itself strong enough to bind the present to the past: that what is needed is a full understanding in every case of what chieftainship has meant and what it can mean in terms of authority and leadership. Certainly it has to acquire a new meaning, for the spheres in which leadership is demanded are no longer the same; the emphasis has shifted from the waging of war to the construction of public works, and the redistribution of revenues received is now a matter not of personal generosity but of budgetary expenditure.

The fundamental necessity for the constructive development of native administration is, as I have suggested, an understanding, not only of the nature of the claim to authority, but of the reasons why authority was in fact obeyed and above all the duties which authority involved. Such an understanding would give a sounder basis than the chance of administrative convenience for the modifications in the chief's status which modern circumstances render necessary. It would make it possible to meet the criticism that Indirect Rule means the maintenance of obsolete tyrannies by the power of alien arms, by curtailing those privileges which, divorced from the responsibility which formerly accompanied them, have in fact become tyrannous. It would dispel the illusion that chiefs can be made the instruments of interests inimical to those of their own people and native political organization remain intact; and the more insidious illusion that in regions where native society has been systematically reduced to dependence on wage-labour for European employers it can be recreated by allotting major administrative functions to hereditary chiefs.

With this understanding there must go a recognition that the chieftainship is not in any society an isolated phenomenon but one of a group of interdependent institutions which combine to determine its sphere of influence. The commands of a native chief are as constitutional as those of a modern parliament – in the sense that he takes for granted the whole social organization of which he is a part. Arbitrary as his power may be in personal matters, it is exercised within the limits of a traditional system of law which it is his duty to uphold and not to modify.

Thus when he is invited by the European government to throw his weight on the side of an innovation desired by them, it is not as an autocrat whose word is law that he makes his influence effective, but either as their recognized instrument or as a person whose general prestige entitles his counsels to respect. Indeed, the belief that fundamental alterations in the structure of any society could be made by a mere word of command rests on a quite unreal conception of the nature of authority and of society itself.

The next step that needs to be taken, in the constructive interpretation of Indirect Rule, is an appreciation of the chieftainship as part of this complex whole which will enable those responsible to judge the value to the society concerned of the modifications that they propose to make through the agency of the native authority.[1] Given such an understanding this system could make possible a more satisfactory development of African society than it has sometimes achieved hitherto, and could refute some of the criticisms brought against it by those most interested in native welfare.

[1] An admirable study of native political institutions from this point of view has been made by Messrs Gordon Brown and Bruce Hutt in their volume, *Anthropology in Action: An Experiment in the Iringa District of the Iringa Province, Tanganyika Territory*, Oxford University Press for the International Institute of African Languages and Cultures, London, 1935.

6

African Chiefs Today[1]

It is a familiar fact that European rule in Africa has set in motion a radical change in African society. In some fields this has not been the result of any deliberate intention. In that of economic development, interest has generally been centred in the immediate problems of production, and the effects upon African institutions of the solutions that have been found for these have been neither planned nor even foreseen. But in the field of politics, European governments have been obliged to define their intentions towards the authorities whom they found already in existence, and here, in theory, there was a clear-cut choice from the start. Either the holders of power in the indigenous societies should be recognized, and utilized as part of an administrative structure of larger scale, or they should be disregarded – their authority be perhaps deliberately destroyed – and replaced by what M Albert Sarraut once called 'new and rectilinear architectures'. The British chose the first course, and this policy has now become inseparably associated with the name of Lugard. I believe that the forthcoming work by Miss Margery Perham will show that what has been called 'Lugardism' in the derogatory sense – I mean the insistence on maintaining traditional authority almost for its own sake – was not Lugard's own philosophy, but that of the successors who were in command during the period when he was away from Nigeria.

The system of administration of African areas that is known popularly as 'Indirect Rule', and more precisely as the Native Authority system, was eventually extended to almost all the British dependencies. The term implies something more than a philosophy of respect for tradition, or a general principle that indigenous authorities should be given administrative

[1] The Lugard Memorial Lecture for 1958, delivered in Brussels on 9 April 1958, on the occasion of the annual Meeting of the Executive Council of the International African Institute; reprinted from *Africa*, **28**, no. 3, July 1958.

responsibilities. The model which was generally copied was the Tanganyika Native Authority Ordinance, a development of Lugard's theme by Sir Donald Cameron. This included specific provisions which make the Native Authority system something very different from the relationship with indigenous rulers that is commonly associated with a protectorate. Under a protectorate the ruler surrenders his external independence but is left more or less free to manage the internal affairs of his territory. Under Lugard and Cameron's system, traditional chiefs or other leaders are recognized as local agents of government and given the title of Native Authority. But their right to exercise authority depends upon this recognition, and recognition may be withdrawn; there is no question of their retaining power because it is inherent in their traditional position. A Native Authority need not be a single individual; in appropriate cases a council of elders may be recognized collectively, or a group of chiefs of areas which are too small to be considered viable by themselves.

The functions of a Native Authority are threefold, and in cases where African chiefs are recognized but do not perform these functions, it may be permissible to speak of Indirect Rule, but it is not correct to speak of the Native Authority system. A Native Authority has judicial, rule-making and financial powers, and in the exercise of all these powers it is subject to external supervision. The grant of financial powers is what made it possible to lay the foundations of local government, in the sense of the allocation of revenues raised in a locality to the provision of services for the direct benefit of those who pay the taxes; and European officials weigh the merit of African chiefs by the interest that they take in such services. The enlightened ruler, in their eyes, is he who introduces the type of local improvement that the government wishes to spread; or, one could put it with less appearance of cynicism, who is interested in the development in his country of institutions appropriate to the twentieth century. Not very many of those rulers who have retained a large degree of independence have spontaneously shown this kind of interest. When this was realized, two alternatives were possible; either all African rulers could be brought under the strict control implied in the Native Authority system, or some other instrument of local government could be developed. In fact, both these courses of action have been tried, sometimes one after the other in the same territory. At the present moment we can see in different British dependencies examples of every stage in the process.

The South African High Commission Territories provide one. The position of the chiefs in Swaziland, Bechuanaland, and Basutoland was defined by treaties made in the nineteenth century, which left them a considerable degree of autonomy. When complaints were made, in the period before the last war, that the development of these territories had been neglected, one step that was taken was to increase control over local administration by limiting this autonomy on the pattern of the Native Authority system. The chiefs resisted this change as long as they could, and by the time it had been made effective the climate of opinion had changed again, and the Native Authority system itself was under fire. Politicians in Europe and Africa were demanding that hereditary rule should be abolished altogether, and replaced by representative local government. When the Ngwato tribe were divided over the marriage of Seretse Khama, the British Government thought the opportune moment had come to do this and so put an end to rivalry between factions; but though there is still no recognized chief of the Ngwato, the people have not been persuaded to elect a council. In the Gold Coast, however, a similar story had a different end. Here too the British Government tried for a long time to induce the chiefs of the coastal area to submit to control in the interests of efficient administration. They refused right up to 1945, and only agreed when they saw that their position was threatened by discontent among their own people. But for them reform was too late to save them from the radical policies introduced by Kwame Nkrumah. In Northern Nigeria, and in East and Central Africa, we are still trying to democratize the government of chiefs without destroying it.

We see today, then, the same opposition within British Africa that used to be regarded as typical of the contrast between the British and the French; the opposition between those who seek to improve what they find and those who prefer to make all new. The forces of African nationalism are on the side of the latter, and where African nationalism has won its first victories, in Ghana and in the Western Region of Nigeria, the status of chiefs has been most conspicuously reduced. Yet in these very territories we see that the chiefs are still a power to be reckoned with, and perhaps all the more so because their place in the formal organization of government has been so drastically diminished. And we sometimes see the same people extolling the traditional political system who at other times are most insistent that chiefs must be subordinated to a popularly elected government.

I do not intend to spend time discussing, in the light of hindsight, whether it was or was not a wise policy to extend the Native Authority system through Africa. One could point to the most successful examples of it as an effective way of providing local services at a time when they could have been provided in no other way. On the other hand, one might ask whether, if Native Authorities had not been recognized in the British territories, political energies there might now be directed to problems of greater ultimate importance than the struggle for power between chiefs and representative leaders. Will a struggle of this kind be unnecessary in the French territories, where the status accorded to chiefs in the colonial system has been so much lower?

The interpretation of history that is popular with some young Africans sees the Native Authority system as a colossal mistake for which they are paying today. I have never heard one of them explain what he considers would have been the wiser policy, but I suspect that they dream of an alternative version of the past in which representative institutions would have been introduced much earlier and in consequence the goal of self-government would also have been reached much sooner.

I would suggest that the assumptions which they make are false in essentially the same way that some of the assumptions made by the architects of the Native Authority system were false. In both cases it is assumed that a political system can be modified by external action in just the direction which is desired. Of the two views, the African is the more naïve – the idea that an authority which is widely accepted can be not only destroyed – which is easy – but immediately replaced by something built on quite different principles; the 'new and rectilinear architectures' of which M. Sarraut spoke were not, in fact, raised in very many places. Behind the Native Authority system was a belief which is in some sense the converse of the African one: the belief, not that everything could be changed, but that nothing would change except under the direction of the European rulers. They, it was held, would guide the chiefs in the way of enlightenment, would remove abuses from the organizations that they found, control the infliction of cruel punishments, limit the demands that chiefs could make on their subjects. Then, having cleaned and polished their instruments, they would turn them to constructive use.

This vision did not take account of the dynamic nature of social relations. It did not recognize that the traditional relationship of chiefs with their subjects had been the result of a continuous inter-action, in which some sort of balance was struck between the claims of the ruler and the expectations of the ruled. There have been a few cases, like that of the Fulani empires, where conquerors had military power strong enough to enforce the submission of conquered peoples. But more often the subjects acquiesced in a rule which they considered to be worth something to them, and the ruler had to approach their ideal of what a chief should be. Certainly this did not prevent him maintaining control over his immediate followers by means of ruthless punishments. Indeed I am not seeking to idealize African tradition, still less to argue that African rulers were in fact democratic, as became fashionable at the time when the Native Authority system was first under fire, and sometimes appears to be so again in Ghana. And when I speak of balance, I do not mean to convey the picture of some delicately poised construction which must not be touched lest its equilibrium be disturbed. I simply mean that authority was accepted as long as obedience was considered to be worth while, but that when this point was passed there were ways of refusing obedience; indivi-duals could transfer their allegiance, larger groups could secede. Less commonly a ruler could be removed by force and a rival installed in his place. The Akan-speaking peoples of Ghana even had a formal procedure for the removal of chiefs; it is not clear how much force was involved in putting this into action in the days when it was still possible to resort to force. But nobody disputed the principle that people should be ruled by a chief, and that he should come from one particular line of descent.

Within this system, as within all social systems, rulers and subjects, nobles and commoners, pursued their own interests to the best of their ability. As long as the traditional African polities were largely self-contained, the principal way in which a com-moner could do this was by pleasing some political superior, and the value of this patronage was one of the most important sources of political power. The populace at large might do no more than acquiesce in the system of rule, or they might regard it as part of a divinely sanctioned order. But the immediate followers of chiefs and their subordinate officials had a clear interest in the maintenance of their power.

The establishment of alien rule had effects upon this system both direct and indirect. Directly, it tilted the balance of power in favour of authority. Certainly governments were greatly concerned to see that chiefs did not exploit their subjects, and that the revenues they collected were devoted to the public welfare, and not merely to their own enrichment. But they also made those chiefs whom they supported almost immune from any effect of popular dissatisfaction. There have indeed been revolts against chiefs under colonial rule, but if they have succeeded it has been indirectly, by calling the attention of the superior government to malpractices. The dual position of the chiefs, between the European government with its specific expectations, and their subjects with quite other expectations, has been discussed by various writers with reference especially to East Africa, notably in a perceptive work by Dr Lloyd Fallers. The officials of the superior government also had a dual role, as the supporters of chiefly authority and the defenders of its subjects against the abuse of authority. They too were not always able to play both roles with success.

In the long run, the indirect effects of colonial rule on the position of the chiefs have been the most extensive. The explanation that chiefs who had government support became indifferent to popular opinion, even in so far as it is true, is too simple to account by itself for the hostility which popular leaders have often shown towards them. We must look not only to the direct relationship of ruler to subjects, but to all the consequences of the fact that the drama of Africa is now being played on a wider stage. This one relationship is no longer of supreme importance. The chief has ceased to be the ultimate source of protection to the humble, aid to the needy, and advancement to the ambitious. It is not simply that the superior government has taken his place, but that the new world offers opportunities which depend on the creation of relationships right outside the traditional system. People can attain success in commerce, or eminence in the professions, without being beholden in any way to their political superiors, and in these fields the chiefs often could not compete with them. In these circumstances, resentment against the rule of chiefs is something more than a protest against injustice, even though it may express itself in that form. It is part of a wider demand: the demand for full participation in the institutions which control the destinies of Africans.

In this situation the chief can be looked at in two ways. He is an individual doing his best to retain the advantages which his status used to bring him, and sometimes coming into conflict with the new leaders in the process, but he is also a symbol, a rallying point for like-minded persons. At different times the chiefs have been found to symbolize different aspects of the complex modern situation. This is the reason why the same chiefs may be objects of hostility at one moment and of vociferous loyalty at the next, and also why the same persons may appear to be successively, or even simultaneously, opponents and supporters of the recognition of hereditary authority.

To some of their subjects, chiefs are the symbol of alien rule simply because they have been entrusted with some responsibilities of government. And when nationalism is militant, they are indeed in a difficult position, since they are part of the machinery for the maintenance of public order, and they have everything to lose if they align themselves with their subjects. It is not surprising that chiefs are usually 'loyal', as it is commonly called; yet it is worth noting that in Nyasaland a few years ago a number of chiefs resigned their office so that they could stand with their people in opposition to the inclusion of their country in a federation with the Rhodesias.

Of course it is an absurd exaggeration to argue as if European supremacy could not have been maintained without the support of the chiefs, and it is also an absurd distortion to identify them with those policies against which the attack on 'colonialism' is commonly directed. These are economic policies, which are implemented through the relations between central governments and the enterprises operating under their protection, outside any field in which the chiefs can act. The only serious criticism that has ever been made of the type of small-scale development that chiefs have been expected to further is that there has been too little of it.

Another way in which the chiefs are made symbols of resentment against foreign rule is in the interpretation that is put on the decisions made by governments when there is a disputed claim to recognition. Since no man advances a claim unless he has some following, some section of the public is bound to be disappointed whoever is recognized; and, as nationalism develops, it comes to be asserted that the official choice is always contrary to the popular will. Sometimes, even in cases where an individual's claim is not challenged, his critics or his enemies may assert that he has been forced upon them by the alien government; but let the government take action against a ruler, however unpopular, and all his subjects will instantly rally to his support.

This phenomenon, which continues to surprise those in authority, can be readily explained. Every hereditary ruler is the supreme symbol of the unity of his people, and therefore, also, of their opposition to outsiders; so an attack on him means much more than the invasion of his personal authority. To the sophisticated among his subjects, whatever their attitude may be towards the person, such an attack is an offence against national sentiment which cannot be tolerated. To the great majority who have little interest in, or comprehension of, the political conflicts of today, their ruler is a part of the fixed order of the universe, and his removal a disaster comparable to the reversal of the seasons. When the British Government withdrew recognition from the Kabaka of Buganda, for one Muganda who had some idea of the matter in dispute there were a thousand who simply felt that they had suffered an appalling injury.

Where there is no external pressure, the politically sophisticated are free to criticize the individual actions of rulers and the hereditary principle itself. But they always have to reckon with the attitude of their simpler fellows, and that is just what I have described in speaking of Buganda.

It is characteristic of African chiefs in all the territories that we are discussing that the political unit which each one symbolizes is only a small division of the political unit which is now recognized, or about to be recognized, as a self-governing State. This fact has created a number of different problems, which depend to some extent on the size of the unit headed by a chief. Ashanti constituted a major division of the Gold Coast under colonial rule. But if it had been merely a British creation, would it have demanded the autonomy of a State in a federated Ghana? Because they were subjects of the Asantehene, the Ashanti formed a collectivity that was more than a geographical expression, and it is because he is aware of this fact that Dr Nkrumah has decreed that Ashanti is to consist in future of eight autonomous divisions subject to no common head. This action, it might be noted, exactly parallels that of the British government some sixty years ago.

In Nigeria at this moment a commission is investigating the numerous demands that have been put forward for the creation of separate States within the three large Regions which at present form the units of the Federation. In some cases the demands appear to be of the type that is stimulated by opposition to external rule; for example, the 'Middle Belt' movement, which seeks to obtain a separate State for the non-Muslim part of the Northern Region, primarily expresses the people's fear of Muslim domination. In other cases, claims are being put forward in the name of language groups; this phenomenon is familiar in European history. Objectively, one can see that if such claims are to have any chance of success, they must relate to larger units than were ever subject to a single ruler. But if the submissions are published it will be interesting to see what part is played in the arguments that are put forward by common allegiance to traditional chiefs.

It is time now to consider the symbolic significance of the chiefs from another point of view. If they stand for the past to people who are proud of that past, they stand for it also in the eyes of people who are impatient to move away from the past into a very different future. This desire is shared today by nationalist politicians and by the people in London who formulate policy for the territories that are still dependent; and to persons in both these categories the authority of the chiefs, if not their person, is the symbol of everything that must be left behind when Africa is modernized. Some journalists too, who, no doubt rightly, see history as a one-way street, describe the attempts of chiefs to assert their position as a 'last stand of reaction'. But some of the conflicts that we see in West Africa today arise from the fact that in the eyes of the same persons the chiefs may be symbols of reaction, symbols of group unity, and symbols of pride in national history. That is why there has been no move to eliminate them from the political system altogether. If the new leaders do not take this step, I think it is not entirely because they are afraid of the strength of the support that the chiefs command. It is also because they themselves see the chiefs – in some aspects – as symbols of national pride; they cannot at the same time repudiate them altogether and assert the value of their own historic tradition. Thus we see in Ghana that when the possibility of establishing a republican form of government is being discussed, it can be asserted that the traditional system in its pristine form was essentially republican.

A place has been found for the chiefs in the new constitutions of Ghana and of the Western Region of Nigeria. In both these countries chiefs are the ceremonial presidents of the elected councils which have replaced the Native Authorities, and up to now they have been allowed to nominate a proportion of the members of these councils, though Dr Nkrumah has now said that each local council is to include only one representative of the chief of the area. In the Western Region, in addition, the legislature is bicameral, and the chamber with powers of revision is a House of Chiefs.

The Eastern Region has always been thought of as the classic case where fully representative government could be introduced without any need for modification to meet the sentiments of traditionalists, because, it was held, there were no chiefs. Indeed it has been regarded as the home of African democracy, where everyone had a voice in all decisions, so that it should be a mere step from the direct to the representative form.

But what do we see in fact in the Eastern Region? A demand for the recognition of chiefs, or at any rate of some kind of traditional leader. It would be easy to explain this away as mere imitation; to say that the Ibo and their neighbours want to claim an institution that appears to be a matter of prestige in other territories. But this is not the whole story. We find now, what an anthropologist might have expected, that the democratic Eastern Region was never democratic as we conceive the Greek City State, in the sense that the voices of all citizens were equal. It was the units of social structure – the small descent groups, each living in its own quarter in town or village – which were equal. No collective decision was taken unless the senior man of each of these groups consented in the name of its members. Sometimes a group might leave the meeting and thus dissociate itself from the decision. This procedure seems to have been carried over into the new parliamentary institutions, where it is less effective, since in this case absentees are bound by the decisions taken in their absence.

When modern representative assemblies are being set up, it is clearly extremely difficult to find a place for the spokesman of every group of this kind, even at the level of local government. Indeed this was tried long ago. In the first days of the introduction of the Native Authority system under Cameron, the principle was followed that the traditional political structure must be utilized *whatever it was*; and for some time assemblies of a hundred or more members were formally responsible for the conduct of business such as the allocation of revenues to local services. But very soon it was found necessary both to reduce the number of councillors and to amalgamate neighbouring units, so as to create economically viable authorities with councils of manageable size. Once this had been done, there was no link with tradition apart from the fact that the council members were reverend elders, and the opinion soon grew up among the officials responsible for the supervision of the councils that the business of a local authority should be in more competent hands. This led them to study the local councils of Kenya, which from their inception have been based on nomination or election and not on any traditional structure, and, taking Kenya as the example, they substituted wholly elected councils for the Native Authorities. The process was set in motion before a representative African Minister took over responsibility for local government. However, the law which authorized it had been examined in advance by a committee of Africans. At that time there does not seem to have been any general feeling that the dignity of traditional authorities must be respected. Evidently they were not thought of as a serious political force, as were those in the Western Region and in Ghana. In these two countries the respect for chiefs appears to be in part derived from religious veneration. Their chiefs used to perform ceremonies on what may be called a national scale; some of them perhaps still do. The head of a kin group, in contrast, is the intermediary only between his own kinsmen and their ancestors. Outside this field he earns the respect generally accorded to age, but no more. It appears, in fine, that the educated persons who were consulted on the original Local Government law did not consider that any account need be taken of traditional leadership.

Yet we now see a reaction. Mr G. I. Jones, who was invited to investigate the question of the due recognition of traditional authorities, refers in his report to 'a general feeling that the principle of representation by election has been carried too far', and this appears to be closely connected with a feeling that the new local council areas do not correspond with social units conscious of common interests. Again we seem to be seeing the importance of the recognized head as the symbol of unity, and the determination of the group whose unity has its roots in the past not to be submerged in new organizations artificially created.

This situation presents a serious problem for the organization of local government, not only in the Eastern Region but also in Ghana and in other territories. Over and over again we find that some section refuses to be included in a wider council, or insists on breaking away from one, on the ground that they are an autonomous political unit headed by their own chief. Now it is not only anthropologists who have remarked on the importance of community sentiment as a stimulus to the activity of local councils, and of community pride as a factor in willingness to contribute to the cost of common services. But if these feelings unite only populations too small to afford any common services, and are strong enough to divide councils representing larger aggregates, they can only hamper the development of effective local government. In time, no doubt, as communications improve, locality by itself will be a basis for community feeling. Meanwhile we must hope that if community pride is appeased by the appointment to councils of persons clothed with traditional authority, this may lead the general public to take more interest in local developments.

The Union of South Africa, to which I now turn, sometimes appears to outsiders like a looking-glass land in which all the trends which are dominant, and seem to be irresistible, farther north are reversed. The attitude reflected in the Union Bantu Authorities Act is a case in point. To liberal South Africans of yesterday, no less than to progressive journalists of today, Bantu chiefs have symbolized reaction, and South Africans have prided themselves on the elected local councils which had been set up in the native areas of the Cape before the end of the last century. At the same time the Native Affairs Department has found it convenient to rely on the traditional chiefs as agents of police power and as channels for the communication of official policy. Also, it was found here, as it has been found since in so many other places, that certain chiefs commanded so much respect that it was not practicable to exclude them from the representative councils which were set up among their people. Thus in Pondoland the Paramount Chiefs of the two major divisions of the country had to be given seats on the councils of the districts in which they lived, and they were also authorized to nominate a proportion of the members of all councils.

But with the advent of the Nationalist Party to power, and the adoption of the policy of *apartheid*, the rule of the chiefs over their people has come to acquire a new significance. Now they are symbols of difference; they embody the theory that Bantu culture is the expression of the specific nature of a people who are destined to be for ever separate from South Africans of European descent. Their responsibilities in the field of local government are to be increased, and they are to exercise these along with councils constituted according to tribal tradition. In this case the ruling group have deliberately chosen to recognize only the divisive forces in African social structure and only the rural populations which still cherish their distinctive traditions, and to disregard the great number, probably now the majority, of Africans who live outside their tribal territory, and for whom it is quite meaningless to say, as was said in the debate on the Bantu Authorities Act, that 'the tribe, the headman and the chief are the basis of their social and political structure'.

What is meant by the return to tradition appears from a speech that the Secretary for Native Affairs made to a meeting of Zulu chiefs soon after the Act was passed. He claimed to be 'adding to the duties of the tribal authorities the all important one of moving with the times and thereby retaining leadership of the community as a whole', and told them 'to deal with community life in all its ramifications just as in the tribal life of old but on a higher level'. Alas, these exhortations ignore the essential factor in the present situation, that the times have changed, and modern community life is not the tribal life of old. The chief can move with the times only up to a point; to go beyond that point would make his own position meaningless. The support which chiefs retain today, and which, I repeat, is strong enough to make them a significant force in politics, comes from the people who do not want to move with the times.

I have spoken of the chiefs as symbols. In every case they are symbols of the differentiation of sectional groups in a complex society, but only in the last of a differentiation which is forced upon one section against its will. The kind of group loyalty which takes a chief as its symbol is often called 'tribalism'. Outside South Africa this word has a derogatory meaning; inside South Africa it is rather ambiguous; officially it means something which is different without being inferior, and which ought to be perpetuated. But some self-appointed mentors of the new African States condemn 'tribalism' and urge Africans to develop a sense of nationhood. In taking this line they forget that every society has, and must have, its internal divisions. Only two features are peculiar in the African political scene at the moment: that the groups which seek to assert their autonomy are unduly small in the context of modern government, and that their unity is symbolized by the recognition of hereditary rulers.

Something must also be said of the chiefs as persons who are seeking, like everyone else, to do the best for themselves in a fluid situation. I am not attempting to deny that the wide popular support which they command sometimes enables them to pursue their own interests rather than the benefit of society at large, even to the point of refusing to obey the law of the land. I am thinking particularly of the situation in Ghana, where the Akan chiefs in the past have derived considerable revenues from their position as the ultimate authorities over unoccupied land. Of course the mystical identification of a chief with the land of his subjects is not peculiar to the Akan-speaking peoples; it is probably universal. But in Ghana the opportunities of turning this position to account have been unusually great, since the country has a highly profitable cash crop, cocoa, and also valuable mineral and timber resources. The cocoa is produced by peasant farmers, many of whom are 'strangers', to use the West African word, in the chiefdoms where they have taken up farms. There is a steady migration of farmers to the better cocoa lands. For cultivation rights they usually pay something to the chief as well as to the right-holder whom they approach directly. Timber and mineral concessions have been granted directly by the chiefs and not by the central government, since the Gold Coast government never claimed any right to dispose of African lands. All these revenues should have been brought to account in the Native Administration treasuries which were set up in Ashanti in 1936 and in the coastal area in 1945. But when the decision was taken to replace the Native Authorities by elected local councils, it appeared that it was not a simple matter to order the transfer of Native Administration assets to the new bodies. In the eyes of those who still revered the chiefs, their position as land authorities was sacred, and to take from them the revenues which were paid in recognition of this position would have been an outrage. A compromise in legal terms was found in the provision that stool lands, as they are called in Ghana, are the property of the traditional entities, the States ruled by the chiefs, but are to be administered on their behalf by the elected councils. This saves the prestige of the chiefs, but it does not alter the fact that the local councils and the chiefs have very different ideas on the question of the allocation of revenues. The councils want to build dispensaries and water storage tanks; the chiefs want to keep up their traditional state, maintain their courtiers and renew the elaborate paraphernalia with which they appear on ceremonial occasions. Their subjects probably want both the water supplies and the paraphernalia; I recall a case in which one of the smaller chiefs near Cape Coast complained to the council that he could not provide the necessary ritual objects for the appropriate yearly ceremony and his people were blaming him for the bad season. Thus there is room for a good deal of friction between hereditary and elected authorities. It has been common form for elected local councils in their first flush of power to cut down what might be called the chief's civil list. In Ghana repeated instructions have had to be given to councils regarding their duty to maintain chiefs, but it is not likely that there will ever be agreement about the proper cash value of maintenance. Already the central government has had to guarantee a payment to chiefs from its own revenues; this too the chiefs have criticized as inadequate.

This is what happens when the chiefs have handed over their revenues, or where the revenues are in any case not large. Where there is more at stake, the conflict arises earlier. The chiefs do not disclose their sources of revenue, or fail to agree with the council on the proportion which they should be allowed to retain; or they try to get in ahead of the council's servants and go on collecting the dues which were formerly paid to them. It appears that the recent suspension from his office of Nana Ofori Atta was the government's answer to his refusal to make over his revenues.

It is quite easy to predict that the chiefs will eventually disappear from the scene, whether or not the governments of independent

Ghana and Nigeria take forcible steps to bring this about. Although, as I hope I have shown, their position differs in many respects from that of a landed aristocracy in Europe, it is equally vulnerable to the forces of modern economic development. Even supposing that representative government does not flourish in the new States, it is unlikely that leadership will revert to the chiefs; it must remain in the hands of people who can organize their following over wider areas than those to which the chiefs are confined by the nature of their position. It may be that sociologists would regard them as constituting a class in modern African society, but they have not shown much ability to combine in defence of their interests.

However, it is too easy simply to say that because they cannot last for ever, they are negligible now. It has been remarked that anthropologists, who study African societies intensively over short periods, exaggerate temporary conflicts. Historians tell us that with their long view they can see how these conflicts will be resolved; so, it seems to follow, the conflicts themselves do not really matter very much. I am reminded of Lord Keynes's remark that 'in the long run we are all dead'. The conflicts that people are living through are the only ones that matter *to them*, and it is a fact that the position of the chiefs is a subject of acute conflict in Ghana, and a live issue in the eastern Region of Nigeria, and nobody has ventured to prophesy what may happen in a self-governing Northern Nigeria, where at present there is no power comparable with that of the great Emirs. We may think we see what the end of the story must be, but that does not enable the actors in the drama to sleep through it and wake up just in time for the dénouement. They have to live through the period of conflict, and it is for them to decide whether the end will be reached through a series of compromises or forced in a violent struggle.

7

Old and New Leadership in Africa[1]

There are now more than twenty African members of the United Nations. Each of these States has at its head a Prime Minister or a President who has gained his position as the result of a popular vote. Some of these men belong to old families. I mean by that that their grandfathers were famous chiefs in the days when African chiefs were independent rulers. Some have no such distinguished ancestry. No one of them owes his present position to the fact that his family is powerful today. The only example of this kind is the Premier of Northern Nigeria, and he is not the head of an independent state but the Premier of a part of a federation. He is the Sardauna of Sokoto, and he is the heir to the throne of a kingdom that is still ruled by a monarch, and a monarch who is very far from being a mere symbolic figurehead. It would take too long to explain why Northern Nigeria is so different from anywhere else in Africa, but this example makes a good starting point for a discussion of the contrast between the old leaders and the new ones.

Before Africa was partitioned among the European nations it was divided up into great numbers of little kingdoms. Not more than half a dozen of these had populations of more than a million. Most of the big ones were in what is now Northern Nigeria, and in the neighbouring territories which used to be colonies of France. Elsewhere chiefs ruled over a few thousands or tens of thousands of subjects. Some peoples recognized no authority beyond the heads of those descent groups which anthropologists call clans.

Some anthropologists have argued that these peoples with no chiefs could not be said to have government. Others say that if government means organizing co-operation for public purposes,

[1] Reprinted from *The Advancement of Science*, March 1962.

then every society has some government. But whether or not you allow that government existed among the peoples who did not recognize chiefs, we are bound to agree that government everywhere meant something very different from what it does today in either the eastern or the western world.

Essentially the purpose of government was to maintain an order of things that was generally supposed to be divinely appointed and to have lasted unchanged for a very long time. Social anthropologists have been taken to task for saying that primitive societies do not change. We are on firmer ground if we say that they do not think they do. Of course they conquered their neighbours if they could, but they thought of this process as just the extension of an existing system, and from the point of view of the conquerors it usually was.

This established order was maintained by punishing offences against it and awarding compensation to the injured. The judicial function of government was by far the most important in the eyes of the governed. There are examples on record where peoples who had no chiefs of their own asked a foreign chief to give them one of his sons to settle their disputes for them.

But the established order was also held to depend upon divine protection, and very commonly the ruler was supposed to be uniquely able to secure this protection, and this was the basis of his right to rule. Hereditary rule was not just a privilege that some family had happened to secure for itself. Let me explain. African religion is based on the cult of ancestor spirits, who can be approached only by their own descendants. The senior living descendant of any line of ancestors was the right man to seek their blessing on the members of the lineage. The ancestors of a chief were concerned not only with their own lineage but with the whole people. But only a member of the chiefly lineage could perform the appropriate rites to secure their blessing; and everything depended upon this blessing – the falling of the rain in due season, and the fertility of crops, of cattle and of men. This is the final justification for hereditary chiefship. Some people also offered other justifications; many of them believed that the first ancestor of the chief had in some sense created the tribe – by having been in the country longest, or by having led the rest of the people from somewhere else to their present home, defeating enemies and performing miracles on the way.

In general, then, what people expected from their rulers was peace and prosperity, and this was conceived in terms of the maintenance of recognized rights and of a general state of well-being. If the rulers organized successful wars, this was even better, especially for the people who got a share of the spoils.

But the colonial rulers of Africa brought with them the idea that governments should do more than keep the peace, and that in Africa governments should be concerned in changing what they found. In the beginning they sought to develop economic resources and improve standards of government, and later they added to this the extension of social services. The colonial idea of improving standards of government was an administrative one. The colonial rulers did not seek to alter the basis of government; they tried to influence the hereditary chiefs to adopt what they considered more enlightened methods and policies. The theory of African government in the first quarter of this century was, first, that there were 'natural rulers' who commanded obedience and, second, that this would always be so. The second part of this theory has turned out not to be true, and nowadays we are constantly reproached because we believed the first part. But the first part *was* true; as long as the African peoples did look to their chiefs as leaders, they resented having other persons appointed to hold authority over them, and in the first years of the colonial era in Africa they certainly never entertained any idea that they ought to choose their rulers by popular vote. People thought the chief was the right man to rule, until the influences that Europeans brought in made them think differently, and in some places, although there is a certain amount of discontent, most of them still do; that is why the heir to a royal throne can be Premier of Northern Nigeria.

The people who predicted that chiefs would always be regarded as the 'natural rulers' did not foresee what would be the consequences of those very changes which the colonial governments wanted the chiefs to further. Colonial governments wanted the chiefs to lead their people in the ways of enlightenment, which of course meant Western ways, and they did not realise that the adoption of new ways must lead to the appearance of new leaders.

The new leaders claim their position on the strength of the popular support that has been shown them. Sometimes this has been shown in the formal procedure of elections, sometimes in the large numbers of people who have been ready, when the new leaders call for it, to join in strikes or other demonstrations. This is what has made these new men first into leaders of political parties and then into heads of states.

To a student of society the interesting question is what sort of people come forward to claim this new kind of leadership, a leadership which is not interested in maintaining an established order but rather in changing things much faster than the colonial governments ever contemplated. Clearly they must be spokesmen for others than themselves, large numbers of people whose aspirations are fixed on the possibilities of a new order; people who have either become impatient with the old, or have realized that so much of the old order has been destroyed that it cannot continue; some of them may be glad of this, others may regret it.

In this situation the traditional leaders are in a nearly impossible position. The more conservative among their followers blame them because they departed from custom. Colonial governments have sought to employ them as bureaucrats, and have been impatient with them just because they are conservative. Those of their subjects who are committed to the idea of progress reproach them because they do not give progressive leadership. Where new leaders have demanded political independence – and this is nearly everywhere – they have thought that governments support traditional rulers on purpose to keep the new men out of the political system. Where governments have treated political movements as subversive, chiefs have been expected to take measures against them, and then their people have regarded them as traitors. Except in the special Nigerian situation that I have mentioned, power is passing from their hands or has already passed.

To whom then has it passed? What kind of men are the leaders of nationalist parties and heads of African states? To a sociologist this does not mean what is their temperament, it means what is their social background. It would be an interesting undertaking for a follower of Sir Lewis Namier to examine the composition of the elected assemblies of some of the newly independent states and make biographies of all their members. In the meantime we have to be content with what we know about the more conspicuous figures.

In the first place, they all have in common some measure of

the education that was originally introduced by the colonial governments. This almost goes without saying; this education is what enabled Africans to enter the new world of the market economy at a higher level than that of unskilled labour. Where literacy is a rare attainment, men who possess it, and gain their livelihood by using it, inevitably become a distinct class with characteristics and interests that separate them from the mass of the population. As time goes on they form organizations to pursue common interests, and in some African territories, such as Northern Rhodesia and Nyasaland, the first germ of political movements is to be found in organizations of this kind.

The first products of colonial schools became clerks and teachers. Later, education expanded to include training for more specialized professions, or else there was a demand for these professions and people went to Europe or America to qualify for them. The most obvious example is medical training at various levels; among the leading political personalities in the West African territories that were formerly French, four have been doctors, including one of the best known, M. Houphouet, Premier of the Ivory Coast, one was trained as a chemist and one as a hospital orderly. In Commonwealth territories we see a doctor as Prime Minister of Sierra Leone, with another doctor in his cabinet. A third is the leader of the nationalist African party in Nyasaland and has just become Minister for Natural Resources. In the ex-French states schoolmasters are also numerous. They include the President and Vice-President of Mali, and that country's Minister of Justice, and six others who are or have been heads of states or heads of governments.

Most colonial governments did not encourage Africans to become lawyers. This was shortsighted, because whatever may be the popular image of a lawyer, no independent state can do without them. But Africans who could afford to go abroad for study have very often studied law. Naturally it is in the more prosperous areas that people make enough money to send their sons abroad, and this may be why we find more lawyers among the prominent men of the cocoa countries – Ghana and Western Nigeria.

Many of the new leaders have been in government service. Patrice Lumumba was a post office clerk; so was Sékou Touré, who is now the President of Guinea. Some have worked for expatriate firms. Some have been in business on their own. In the former French territories one or two priests have been prominent; one of these is now president of the Congo Republic whose capital is at Brazzaville.

I have been placing these new leaders in categories according to their jobs. There are other ways of dividing them. You can divide them by generation, or by the place where they have got their education, in other words whether they have gone abroad for it. To some extent these categories coincide, since young Africans today have many more opportunities to study abroad than their fathers had.

The essence of the contrast between the younger and the older generation of new Africans is that the younger are in more of a hurry. This is a platitude that could be applied to the contrast of generations all over the world. But in the African context, it is not a mere truism. Other factors beside the impatience of youth have influenced the attitudes of the younger generation. Some writers on this subject attach prime importance to the experience of life abroad, particularly in America. African students there have become conscious of their common interests as Africans. On the one hand they have realized that racial discrimination is not confined to Africa, and on the other they have come into contact with liberal opinions of different shades which provide them with arguments against discrimination. The knowledge that this liberal opinion exists has greatly, and of course rightly, increased the confidence of the younger generation of African leaders in their demand for a new order of things. If I do not emphasize the effect of the attainment of independence by so many African territories on those which are not yet independent, it is because I am trying to consider influences that go back rather further in time. The same reason accounts for my emphasis on study in America as an influence on English-speaking Africans.

The new leaders in earlier generations were less radical in their demands than those of today. Some were even not radical at all. Partly this was because they had not conceived the possibility of a demand for independence and for some kind of new political system. Partly it was because more of them were satisfied with the place they had achieved in the colonial society. In some places another reason was that they were themselves closely connected with the traditional leaders. I have the Gold Coast particularly in mind. The first educated generation were either members of chiefly families or their retainers, and the first approximation to a political party was the Aborigines Rights Protection Society, which fought to protect the position of the chiefs against encroachment by the colonial government. The leaders of the first educated *élite* wrote manuals of customary law. They defended the older, hereditary leaders against anyone who should attempt to undermine their position. They were replaced, first by the United Gold Coast Convention, and then by Nkrumah's Convention People's Party which broke away from the latter. This party, like most contemporary ones, sought its support among the masses, and found its leaders among young men who had no standing in the traditional rank system and little hope of obtaining any in the colonial one. These younger men resented the privileged position of the traditional leaders, and, as I have indicated, regarded their acquiescence in – what colonial governments call loyalty to – the colonial régime as a betrayal of the African populations. The same attitude was expressed in a book written while he was in England by Obafemi Awolowo, who later became the first Premier of the Western Region of Nigeria. Awolowo had a stronger case, because in Nigeria the traditional chiefs were much more explicitly employed as agents of government policy; he argued that a corrupt and anachronistic type of government was being imposed on the Nigerian peoples in the interests of colonial rule.

A more up-to-date illustration comes from Nyasaland. I quote it because I have recently been in that country. You can see the cleavage of the generations very clearly there, and also the attitude of the new generation towards the traditional leadership. The nationalist party there grew out of a welfare organization of civil servants, of the kind that I mentioned at the beginning of this paper. At the same time that this body was formed, councils of traditional Native Authorities were set up with the idea that the chiefs were the right men to speak for African public opinion. Later, some persons who were not chiefs were brought into these councils. When African representatives were first brought into the Legislature they were elected by these councils. They chose five men, all members of the nationalist party, three middle-aged and two young, who very clearly illustrated the difference between the generations. Of the three elders, one had been head clerk on a large estate and had then started cash farming on his own, one was a teacher and one had worked on a newspaper. The two young men had both studied in African universities outside Nyasaland. One had been an Administrative Assistant, the first African in Nyasaland to attain this rank; the other had been a teacher.

The seniors sought to gain their ends by co-operation with the Nyasaland government, the juniors by defying the government. It was the juniors who persuaded Dr. Hastings Banda to come home and lead a militant independence campaign, and since he went back all the positions of control in the party have passed to the younger generation and the former leaders have left it.

So we can see leadership passing from the hereditary rulers to a first and then a second generation of men who have achieved their position through the prestige that they have won for themselves. The first generation have a modicum of education and they had had a good deal of experience before they appeared on the wider political stage. The second have had much more advanced education but less experience of life.

In the contest for leadership in the field of party politics, the older generation seem often to have lost significance. But the traditional rulers are still part of the picture. The part they play is very different in different places. In Northern Nigeria they are still almost the only leaders, and the big Emirs command a hierarchy of subordinates who seem likely to protect them for some time against the subversive effect of democratic ideas. The rulers in Northern Nigeria have not had the experience of being called upon to exercise their authority on behalf of a foreign government against subversive movements. Their country has attained independence while they are still firmly in power, and they will have to deal in their own way with the challenges that must eventually confront them.

The other chiefs have been placed in the difficult position that I have described. They have had to choose between opposing nationalist movements and losing the government recognition on which they now depend. In the circumstances of today they are driven to appear as traitors to one side or the other. To take the example of Nyasaland again, it is interesting to see how in the recent elections the European political party sought to woo the chiefs with promises of higher status and better pay. In this situation the conservatism of attachment to the old order of African custom becomes most unhappily mixed up with the conservatism of the *status quo* created under European rule.

This is one of the many aspects of African society where we are seeing compressed into a few years the changes that took centuries in Europe. But we are constantly reminded – and not least by Africans – that the new Africa is not aiming at imitating Europe in every detail. We can be sure now that monarchical rule will not be regarded as an essential part of the African personality. But the solidarity of the peoples who have the tradition of allegiance to a common chief is still very strong, and it is possible that in some countries the new African governments may use chiefs as their agents in much the same way as the colonial rulers did.

8

Race, Tribalism and Nationalism in Africa[1]

The political problems of Africa are commonly discussed in terms of relations between races. The British dependencies in particular are popularly conceived as falling into two classes – the homogeneous and the multi-racial. Those of the west are described as homogeneous; in this context the word means that there is no non-African population permanently settled there, claiming a stake in the country and a voice in political decisions. In Eastern, Central and Southern Africa, all the larger territories have settled populations of relatively recent immigrants, whose origins are in Europe or Asia. In these territories there is marked political opposition between Africans and non-Africans, and also between the immigrant populations of different origin, and it is here that plans for political advance have met with the most serious difficulties. In West Africa, British governments have been able to negotiate with leaders claiming to speak for whole territories, or at least large geographical regions. But in East Africa the people who put forward claims represent sections defined by their ethnic origin, and usually the claims of each section are incompatible with those of the others. Each of them is looking ahead to the position that it hopes to hold in a future independent state, and seeking to secure that position in advance.

In West Africa, sectional claims have been put forward, but this has not seriously impeded the process of transition towards self-government. There have been some minor difficulties. For example, Sierra Leone has a largely westernized population in Freetown and the neighbourhood, descended from the freed slaves who were settled there in the eighteenth century; they are known as the

[1] Paper delivered at a joint conference of the Royal Anthropological Institute and the Institute of Race Relations in 1959; reprinted from *Man, Race and Darwin* (P. Mason, ed.), 1960, London.

Creoles. The Creoles resisted the extension of the vote to the peoples of the interior, which had the effect of making them a minority; they used just the kind of arguments which might be used by Sir Roy Welensky. However, in general the peoples of the West African territories have seemed to be united as they passed through the preliminary stages towards self-government. But when self-government is round the corner, some of them do begin to wonder who is going to do the governing, and whether power will be in the hands of a section of the total population whom they regard as alien to themselves. This kind of opposition can appear at the lowest level of the political structure, and between quite small groups. In local government, it is creating a rather paradoxical situation both in Ghana and Nigeria. Local government experts keep telling the public how important it is to create large local authorities, with revenues to pay for services of a high standard. But on the ground a tiny village will refuse to be joined in the same council with a larger neighbour, because it regards the people of the neighbouring village as strangers who cannot be trusted to take its interests into account.

This kind of local particularism is sometimes called 'tribalism'. Africans think this word is derogatory, and the people who use it often mean it to be so. If we are talking of political units of small size, which once were subject to no control from outside, the only name for them is 'tribe'. Nowadays these are divisions of larger units, which are seeking to become nations, or claiming that they are so. But when the word 'tribalism' is used, it nearly always implies a narrowness of outlook which is unworthy of people claiming nationhood, and since it is never used in relation to European populations, it inevitably implies something that Europe has grown beyond. We do not refer to the Scots or the Welsh as tribes, and so when they demand home rule we cannot logically call this tribalism. But their demand is not so very different from the demand of the Ashanti in Ghana for a federal constitution in which their territory would be one state. The Ashanti did not get what they wanted, and the sad sequel was that they were too proud to be satisfied with half measures, and ended up with nothing at all.

Nigeria, on the other hand, seemed destined to be a federation, if only by reason of its vast extent. Indeed in this case the foundations of a federal constitution were laid with the aim of decentralizing the administration rather than with the intention of meeting local feelings. But the local feelings have turned out to be very definitely there. It is true that Dr Azikiwe's party, the National Council of Nigeria and the Cameroons, which was the first expression of nationalism in the country, took as its slogan 'One Nigeria'. It is true too that this party does have adherents outside the Ibo country where it started. But the other two large parties draw their support primarily from geographical areas, and not from classes or groups with a common interest which could extend across these frontiers. This situation seems likely to make it difficult to develop federal parties with common policies, or even one federal party; and the logical result of this seems to be that the federal government must be dominated by the Northern People's Congress because the North has the largest number of seats. And as the Northern People's Congress has the support of the Emirs, this may create a situation in which the more westernized elements in the South feel that their advance is being hindered by the backward North. This situation might encourage the development of a single progressive party, and such a party would certainly win adherents in the North. But it might also lead to a division of the Federation.

Up to now what we have seen is a series of demands, like that of the Ashanti in Ghana, for the carving out of new autonomous units from the existing Regions. These demands provided the most contentious issue in the last stages of discussion of the Nigerian constitution.

A number of different methods, short of the division of the Federation into smaller units, have been proposed to allay the fears of these minorities. For the Ijaws who live in the swamps of the Niger Delta, divided between the Eastern and Western Regions, the solution is to treat them as a special area for which development schemes are to be financed both by regional and federal governments. For the Edo-speaking people in the West and the Efiks of Calabar in the East, there are to be advisory councils, each presided over by a Minister with the affairs of this minority as his sole responsibility. In addition steps have been taken to secure the impartiality of the police force. The commission which examined this question laid much emphasis on the principles of democratic government as the most important safeguard. It seems, however, that in some cases at least, the feeling that people of common culture should in some way be recognized as a political entity has not been satisfied. Mr Awolowo in particular is not content with the decision to leave two provinces with a large Yoruba-speaking population in the Northern Region.

What we see in West Africa is an extreme development of local loyalties. We are talking about people for whom travel has been difficult until very recently, so that they still think of near neighbours as foreigners. They derive their sense of unity from a tradition of common loyalty to a chief, a tradition of attachment to an area of land, a common name and sometimes a language which is different from that of their neighbours. Like everyone else, they cannot tolerate having their lives controlled by outsiders. As long as the outsiders are British, they protest along with their neighbours. But when independence is near, they find that it is not likely to be 'freedom' in the sense of unlimited control of their own destinies. Hence there arise the kind of oppositions that I have been describing; in each case some territorial section is asking for autonomy, and usually for a greater degree of autonomy than the government of the whole political unit is willing to concede.

Now as long as people stay in the place which their society as a whole regards as 'theirs', the problems that the divisions between them create may be met by devices giving them local autonomy; though if we are to go by the present attitude of the Ghana government, we may infer that newly independent rulers will prefer not to give such open recognition to breaches in their national unity. But new questions arise when people begin to move about – the questions that can be summed up in the one big question, 'Whose country is it?'

This question is associated with the distribution of the land between the different major groups that has been made in the so-called 'White Men's Countries'. This is not a territorial division in the sense in which I have been using the words, because the African populations are not expected to live their whole lives in the place that has been allotted to them. On the contrary, they are expected to spend a large part of their working lives providing the labour which is required in the non-African area.

Africans resent a system which makes them second-class citizens in countries which it is *prima facie* reasonable to call 'theirs'. But here too we are dealing with a situation that is not peculiar to the relations between Europeans and non-Europeans. It has close parallels, in similar circumstances, in the relations between Africans who belong to different ethnic groups.

Many kinds of economic development – perhaps all kinds – create a demand for labour that cannot be supplied without a redistribution of the population. We are most familiar with this phenomenon in the form of migration from rural to urban areas. In Africa it takes this form particularly in the great mining areas, but there is also a new demand for wage-labour in every place where commercial farming has been introduced. One such place which is often conspicuous in the news is the Highland area of Kenya. Here, only Europeans can obtain rights in land, but African labourers are allowed to live there as long as they are employed by their European landlord, but no longer. This is the major grievance of the Kikuyu, who claim that a large part of the White Highlands has been carved out of their tribal lands. Where land has not been allocated to non-native use by an alien government, we do not find peoples claiming that their land has been taken from them, but we may find a closely similar relationship between employers and labourers. After all, not all the labour tenants in the White Highlands are Kikuyu; some of them belong to tribes which have no claim to the land on which they are living as tenants. Such people are in very much the same position as the immigrants into Uganda who work on the coffee or cotton farms of Ganda landowners. The Ganda too want the immigrants to stay in their country only as long as they are working; the Ganda too complain that you can't get a good day's work out of these foreigners; the Ganda too exclude them, or try to, from any share in political representation; the Ganda too describe the labourers as 'dirty people', 'lazy', 'not really civilized', 'we couldn't let our daughters marry them'. Now if a Ganda girl were to marry an immigrant she might have to put up with a much lower standard of living than if she married a Ganda, but her children would not have physical characteristics that proclaimed their origin at once. So it is clear that it is not necessarily the so-called 'racial' physical characteristics of an out-group which leads an in-group to disapprove of marriage with them.

We see in the Ganda an attitude which directly corresponds to that of the Kenya settler, and indeed of the South African nationalists. It is the attitude of an in-group resisting the claims of an out-group to a share in its corporate interests – in this case, land ownership and political rights. Arguments based on 'racial' differences do no more than buttress the antagonism of interests; and it is particularly striking to find the arguments against inter-marriage, and the attribution of innate characteristics, bandied about in circumstances where those experts who divide humanity into races would see no difference between the antagonists.

The real reason why 'race' looms so large in the territories of East and Central Africa is that identification with one of the three major divisions is held to imply a fixed position in the social structure. Of course it is the European immigrants who have been able to establish this distribution by virtue of the immense technical superiority with which they came to Africa, and without which the economic development of the continent would not have been possible. At the time when this development began they alone could have directed it. This is a historical fact, but to recognize it does not necessarily involve one in accepting the claim which some of them make to be repaid by a permanent position of privilege. This is the claim that is now being disputed by the Asians and the Africans. They too have made indispensable contributions to the economic development of their country – the Indians in capital and skills, and the Africans in labour. They are no longer willing to accept as fixed the distribution of economic functions and of political power which the Europeans regard as appropriate.

In this situation the different groups have much rational and specific reason to be afraid of one another's intentions, because there are spheres in which they really are competitive. It is a fact that any redistribution of political power or of economic functions must injure the immediate interests of those who gain most from the *status quo*. In the economic field there is conflict over the distribution of land and over access to skilled employment. The dominant minority are on the defensive; they are afraid of the kind of policy that is foreshadowed in the claims of some African leaders, such as the Mau Mau promise to restore to the Kikuyu what they think of always as the land stolen from them. But the Africans are afraid too; they do not think they have nothing to lose but their chains, because they believe that they can still lose what land is left to them. This is the ever-present fear of Africans in the

Federation of Rhodesia and Nyasaland, and there are circumstances that lend colour to it.

A deposit of emeralds was found in a native area in Southern Rhodesia not long ago; most people would think it reasonable that this should be developed, but this cannot be done without displacing some Africans. Others have been moved from land where, wittingly or not, they had settled outside the boundaries allotted to them; others had their land flooded by the Kariba Dam. It is true that Africans can expect some share in the developments which the dam will make possible, but it is also true that they will not be the principal beneficiaries, and it is only too likely that, through nobody's fault, the people who have been dispossessed will not benefit at all. In Northern Rhodesia some years ago it was proposed to give the status of Native Trust Land to all the land that had not been actually allocated to Europeans; but the local European population refused to have included in the Native Trust Land the areas which it seemed possible that Europeans might want to take up in the future. In Nyasaland the Africans' principal reason against joining the Federation was their fear that the change of status would lead to the loss of their land. In all the territories with a settled European population Africans believe that all Europeans want more and more land; and even in Uganda the most acute difficulties have arisen when the government sought to acquire land for unexceptionable purposes such as industrial development or the building of the East African University College. Actually it is only in Kenya that Europeans feel that land rights as such are important among the privileges to be defended. They defend their claim to the White Highlands on the ground that they farm better than Africans would, and by doing so have made Kenya what it is; and this is true of those European farmers who do farm better.

But in the industrialized areas the privilege that is at stake is that of access to skilled employment, and here it is only the Europeans who are on the defensive. Here lines are drawn not on the map but on pay-sheets and schedules of categories of employment, and since it has come to be taken for granted that any job is *either* a white man's *or* a black man's, the question that is argued is how many of the lower rungs of the ladder the European employees will leave to the Africans. In Britain Secretaries of State reiterate that we do not stand for a colour bar; but if the European mineworkers on the Copperbelt are willing to go on strike for eight weeks over a proposal to schedule nine types of job as unskilled, that kind of protestation does not carry much weight. Nevertheless, the ceiling for the African miner has been raised a little.

But it is in the political field that in-group sentiments and stereotypes can be invoked to rally persons who are not directly faced with a challenge to their own position. Where material interests are concerned, the opposition is not always as clear-cut as it is made out to be; employers of labour are much less enthusiastic about the industrial colour bar than are skilled workers, and in the Union they are wholly opposed to the doctrine of *apartheid* as preached by Dr Verwoerd. In the Union, too, local authorities are not always pleased to raise the rates so as to rehouse thousands of people in neatly delimited 'racial' zones. In Central Africa there are divisions among the Africans themselves between those who can hope to gain by the opening to them of new jobs and those who cannot. Some European trade unionists think they can make terms with African labour as the best way of protecting themselves. But when the question at issue is the weight of different voices in determining national policy, almost everyone sees the situation in terms of 'us or them'. It is true that some of the present holders of power go further than others in the concessions that they are willing to make to 'them'. But they all think equally in stereotypes and slogans. Government, they say, must be in responsible hands, and with this everyone will agree. But when they equate the word 'responsible' with the word 'civilized' one becomes more sceptical, since most people used the word 'civilized' to mean 'just like us'.

On the other side, that of the majority with little or no share in power, the slogans are borrowed from the holders of power. African leaders are familiar with the reasons why Europeans claim universal franchise as a right, and they naturally question the arguments that are used to deny it to Africans. I do not dispute that the immediate introduction of unqualified arithmetical democracy into East and Central Africa might have disastrous consequences, or even that it may be impracticable as a political system in countries as deeply divided as these territories are. I merely say that it naturally appeals to the populations whose numbers would give them predominant power under such a system.

All kinds of constitutional experiment are being tried in these territories. Some of the promoters see these experiments as stages on the way to universal suffrage, or at least to a point where the African voice will be as loud as that of the European. Some in the territories concerned see them as the most they are willing to concede. Too many see them as already conceding too much. To all Africans the concessions seem grudging and inadequate. Not all African leaders are demanding immediate universal suffrage, but they all want more than they are being offered.

In one form of constitution-building, representation is allotted on a communal basis, to use a word borrowed from India, where it makes more sense than it does in Africa. It has been announced as the aim of British policy that no one race should be in a position to dominate the others, and in Tanganyika this has been implemented by creating a legislature made up in equal numbers of representatives of the three major 'races'. In Kenya both Europeans and Africans have demanded half the total of representative seats; the present distribution does not give this proportion to either.[1]

At the same time attempts are being made in various ways to get away from communal voting. In the Rhodesias this has been done by creating a common electoral roll for Europeans and Africans, with educational and property qualifications for the latter. It has been calculated that if all the Africans who were qualified had registered and voted, they would have been a force to reckon with, at any rate in some constituencies. But since less than two thousand actually did, they were merely swamped by the European vote.

The move away from communal voting is intended to promote that 'partnership' between the races which Rhodesia has proclaimed as the aim of the Federation. It is obvious that communal voting encourages the emergence of candidates who seek votes on the basis of the interest of one 'race' in competition with the others, and it is argued that parties representing interest groups which cut across these divisions can only develop if candidates have to obtain support from members of all races. But in Rhodesia even this argument can be used to block any increase in the political weight accorded to Africans. 'Merit and not race' is a fine maxim if you can find an impartial judge of merit; where it is tacitly assumed that merit is the monopoly of Europeans, there are good grounds for

[1] Constitutional changes are in progress in both Kenya and Tanganyika.

the arrangement in the new constitution for Northern Rhodesia, that one post of Minister and one of Assistant Minister should be reserved for Africans, as the only way to enable Africans to get their foot on the ladder. But even this has been indignantly denounced as 'racialism'.

Just as Africans have ignored elections in the Federation, so they boycotted an arrangement in Kenya whereby twelve members of the legislature were to be elected by all the existing members voting together. Here too their reason was that European votes – counting those of the Official Members – would have dominated the choice. Yet they had enough votes to affect the issue, if they had used them.

Some African nationalists seem to hold that intransigence must win in the end; and to hold also that the opposition between 'them' and 'us' is irreconcilable – that no African who can gain the votes of Europeans can be a true spokesman of African interests.

The independence of Ghana is a symbol and a portent to both sides in this political contest. To the Africans it stands for 'what *we* could do'. To the Europeans every false step, every departure from the pure principles of democracy, is an example of 'the kind of thing *they* do'; but if these principles are violated a good deal nearer home, that is different. It has also given a new argument to the Rhodesian nationalists, if that is the right name for those who are demanding full self-government for the Federation: the argument that Rhodesia is not 'more backward' than Ghana. People who argue on these lines ignore the fact that the maintenance of Colonial Office control in Central Africa has never been justified on the ground of the 'backwardness' of the European population; but the argument is immensely effective as a slogan.

Governments in Central Africa are so afraid of the influence of independent Ghana that they will not even allow the leader of the Ghanaian opposition to enter their territory. It is true that the very existence of Ghana is an encouragement to Africans elsewhere; perhaps too much of an encouragement, since Ghana can give them no more than moral aid and comfort. But in this sphere Ghanaians will give all they can.

The All-African Peoples' Conference that was held in December, 1958, in Accra and held another meeting in 1960 in Addis Ababa set up a permanent organization to 'accelerate the end of imperialism' and 'mobilize world opinion against injustices to Africans'.

What is perhaps more interesting, however, is its avowed aim of working towards a 'United States of Africa'. Here again we see how the sense of unity is created by the sense of opposition, and again we must ask whether such a high ambition will prove possible of achievement when the time comes to ask which voices will call the tune. Again we see the paradox of the discrepancy between the wide horizons of African leaders and the narrow ones of their followers; of course this is not confined to Africa, but the leaders of older states do not usually set their sights so high. But the idea of uniting the new African states as they emerge is not a mere idealistic dream; it would be very desirable for material reasons that they could be organized into larger units. Most African leaders realize how slender their resources are, and several of them look in this direction for their salvation. The declaration of union between Ghana and Guinea was a serious attempt to set the process going; Mr Nkrumah has indicated that the constitution of the union will be one to which other African states can adhere. Some of the territories in the French *communauté* are seeking to combine in federations that would be more genuinely federal than the system in which they were grouped in the past. In Central Africa Dr Hastings Banda sees as the way for Nyasaland to escape from federation with the Rhodesias the creation of a new federation with Tanganyika, the Trust Territory of Ruanda-Urundi, the predominantly African parts of Northern Rhodesia, and eventually Kenya. This is the most visionary of all the proposals, and it has already been repudiated by the African National Congress in Northern Rhodesia. It will be one of the most interesting questions for the future to see whether such combinations can be built up and maintained by neighbours who have so recently been strangers.

9

Self-Government or Good Government?[1]

One of the most remarkable features of the last few years has been the change in the relations between colonial territories and the metropolitan powers responsible for their government. In some cases these changes have been brought about by force, where peoples who had been subject to Japanese occupation seized the opportunity created by the interregnum after the Japanese surrender to establish their own governments claiming to be recognized as independent. This occurred in Indo-China and in the Netherlands Indies. In Indo-China the demands of the local leaders went far beyond anything that had been contemplated in France before the war, though in 1945 the French Provisional Government had announced its intention to establish a federal relationship with Indo-China, itself already nominally a 'federation' of colonies and protectorates. The Dutch on the other hand had been contemplating proposals for fuller self-government for the Indies before the war, but none of the plans envisaged then gave the degree of independence claimed by the Indonesian Republic. In both these territories the metropolitan power has found it necessary to use armed force to assert a position which it is not prepared to give up; in both cases it is uncertain whether the former rulers may not have to surrender even what seems to them to be the essential minimum of control.

In India there was no armed conflict. The aim of ultimate independence had long been accepted in Britain, and differences of opinion turned on the question whether the time was ripe. Yet, when the decision to withdraw was finally taken, perhaps the determining consideration was that the British position in India could not be maintained without the use of armed force on a scale

[1] Reprinted from *World Affairs*, vol. 2 (new series), 1948.

greater than was held to be morally justifiable. The situation was similar in Burma.

Yet the history of recent years is not simply a history of reluctant concession to force. The feeling that the rule of any people by a government alien to it and not responsible to it is very hard to justify, and indeed can only be justified in so far as it prepares for its own extinction, is coming to be more and more widely held; and that not only among the subjects of this rule and the peoples of nations which, having themselves few or no overseas territories, are quicker to see the defects of 'imperialism' than to regard it as a historical necessity, but by public opinion in the nations which have colonies. The response to this feeling in British colonial policy has been an overhaul of the constitution of all the colonies and their modification so as greatly to increase the weight given to representatives of local opinion. Ceylon now has full Dominion status. Malta has responsible government in internal affairs. The legislature with a majority of unofficial members is now the rule rather than the exception, in contrast to the system that was general before the war, under which a majority of the members were official, and measures could be carried at any time by the votes of the official bloc. With the unofficial majority a Government Bill can be defeated on the floor of the House. Since this system is still short of full responsible government, and the executive is not removable by an adverse vote in the legislature, the Governor still retains power, through the right of certification, to enact measures deemed essential. Though some colonial nationalists interpret this provision as nullifying the rights conceded to them, it is recognised that the power of certification exists only for exceptional cases of absolute necessity. In general, unofficial representation has been increased and included in Executive as well as Legislative Councils, and the franchise has been extended. The two major West African colonies now have unofficial African majorities, and in East and Central Africa there are, or will be shortly, African members in all the Legislative Councils.

The process that has been set on foot must go on with increasing momentum. There are enough historical examples to show that the intermediate stages on the way to self-government are regarded by the peoples concerned always as something more than positions to be consolidated, always as springboards for the next advance.

What are the consequences likely to be, for the world and for the peoples most directly concerned? Can one draw up a balance sheet of advantages and disadvantages? Or is the process one of pure advantage, an instance of that 'progress' in which our grandparents had so much more confidence than we have?

We have all asserted, over and over again, that good government is no substitute for self-government, and where we ourselves are concerned we have no doubt that it is true. Hence the uneasiness of our conscience towards the colonial peoples subject to our rule. Have we then found here an absolute in the field of politics – a principle that holds good without qualifications in any time or place? If so, why should not all the imperial powers withdraw at once from their dependencies? The most insistent of their critics have not asked for this, though in the case of the Far Eastern colonies America would not allow her troops to take part in the re-establishment of the colonial governments. In Africa ten-year time-limits have sometimes been mentioned.

This suggests qualifications of the principle. Are there circumstances in which independence would not be an improvement on colonial rule? Some colonial nationalists would retort with an appeal to the absolute; material conditions may in some ways deteriorate, but this is of no account in comparison with the value of freedom itself. Others would assert that if in some respects – notably the level of material resources and social services – colonial territories are at a lower level than the independent nations, this is actually a result of their colonial status, and emancipation is the remedy.

There is one wholly logical position, if one has the courage to accept it. It is the one summed up in the statement that 'Everyone has the right to be miserable in his own way'. If a people prefer autocracy to democracy, arbitrary justice to the rule of law, contaminated water to drains, poverty with leisure to hard work and higher real incomes, it is no one else's business. From this position one can look on at communal massacres, dacoity, famine or near famine, and reflect that whatever sufferings these events may cause to however many individuals, they are as nothing to the recognition of the principle that every people has the right to conduct its own affairs in its own way. One may regret these events, but one has no right to invoke the argument that under colonial rule they would not have occurred; and, indeed, one is obliged to admit that independent States have allowed or caused equally great sufferings to as many or more individuals among their own subjects and those of their neighbours. One must set against them, too, that sense of a new dignity, of an advance in human status, that observers tell us is apparent in the very bearing of the ordinary man in those countries which have recently won independence.

But is this the whole story? Is there nothing but complacency and hypocrisy – self-deception and the deception of others – in the belief that colonial rule brought some amelioration to the conditions of its subjects? Was the reluctance of some sections of opinion in Britain to see that happening in India which has happened a mere cloak for economic and military interest?

Undoubtedly the conception of 'the white man's burden' has been invoked to give a colour of public-spirited self-sacrifice to many activities undertaken out of sheer self-interest. The argument that it is a moral duty to make two blades of grass grow where one grew before is the basis even today of the claim that the European entrepreneur in the colonies has a moral right to conditions in which he can make a profit. While it is true that few colonial enterprises have yielded large profits, that is a very different thing from saying that they were undertaken solely in a spirit of service to humanity. It would be more honest to admit that the commercial motive in the acquisition and retention of colonies has always been self-interested – which is not the same as to say anti-social – whether or not the colonies have gained by its working out.

Without accepting the crude theory that colonial peoples as a whole have been 'exploited' for the benefit of the metropolitan powers, one can see certain respects in which it is quite clear that the colonies have been at a disadvantage through the fact that trade policy is not determined locally and that control of the most important business enterprise is outside the colony. Tariff policies are decided by the metropolitan powers primarily in their own interests. This will be less easy in the case of colonial legislatures with an unofficial majority, unless these questions are considered important enough to necessitate the use of the Governor's power of certification. The business firms, with whom alone members of the local population could have learnt the techniques of management, have given very little opportunity to such young men. They are often able to establish a monopoly of import trade and control retail prices. They have shown little benevolence towards the development of local industries which might compete with their imports, if they have not actively opposed it. In an age where it is accepted that a share of the profits of enterprise is taken by the State for expenditure in the general interests of the community, far too large a part of this share has been taken by the treasuries of the metropolitan powers.

And yet they have introduced capital into the colonies, and increased their productivity, and with it their national income and the resources, small as they have been, available for the provision of social services.

So we return to the question whether, for the colonial peoples, the right to be miserable in their own way involves their continuance at the standard of life which had been attained in the days of subsistence or barter economy. The appeal to this right is valid against those who liked to believe they were performing a noble action in teaching lazy peoples the dignity of labour. Today there are still some people in many colonies whose lives have changed little in the past sixty years and who are not interested in what we should consider improvement. But colonial nationalism is not the assertion of *their* point of view. On the contrary, their existence is one of the counts in the indictment of the colonial ruler by the colonial nationalists. It proves, they say, the hollowness of such metaphors as 'trusteeship' or even 'partnership'. Advancement, progress, is their aim, that progress which, they argue, has been denied them up till now.

The progress sought is in material standards – better social services, higher individual incomes. It depends therefore on an increasing national income, and this depends on higher productivity, and this in turn on the provision of capital. The capital must come from outside because the margin of resources available within the colonies is not sufficient to supply what would be necessary for a really substantial increase in productivity. In the British colonies it has been provided on a very limited scale since 1940 from the Colonial Development and Welfare Vote, and the Overseas Development Corporation created in 1947 is intended to supply it on a much larger scale for purely economic purposes. Although these arrangements involve no element of profit for the private investor, they are yet regarded with a certain suspicion by colonial nationalists, who see in them a perpetuation of external control.

Here we come to the real dilemma. Colonial leaders desire something which it is entirely impossible that they should produce for themselves. While their people remain in their dependent position, the metropolitan powers may provide this – not from altruism but from mixed motives: the recognition that eventual independence is inevitable and will be meaningless if it has not a sound economic foundation, the desire to increase the total of world trade, an urgent demand in the metropolitan country for a particular commodity.

When the present colonies are free, however, there will be only two alternatives. Either they will by that time have attained a level of productivity at which capital for further development can be supplied from local saving – which does not seem very likely – or they will have to obtain it from abroad on ordinary commercial terms. For those colonies which have already become independent only the second alternative is available. It has been approached in various ways. The Philippines – not without strong local opposition – have accorded special privileges to United States capital. The Indonesian Republic at one time expressed its readiness to welcome the return of Dutch enterprise to Java. In Burma foreign capital is to be expropriated.

The most likely general prognostic seems to be a policy of economic nationalism, in the sense of heavy taxation of foreign firms and the imposition of various restrictive conditions on them – a policy which is not calculated to attract new capital. A distinguished West Indian economist has expressed the view that, in the absence of sufficient judgment to hit the perfect mean, it is better to accept the investment of capital on terms which will attract it – 'exploitation' if you like – than to impose restrictions which can only act as a deterrent to investors. But it does not seem likely that many people in the colonies will listen to him.

Capital is indispensable to the aims of the colonial nationalists. A factor about which one cannot speak with the same certainty is efficiency. Efficiency, precision, surgical asepsis, the nut fitting the bolt, the airman making his rendezvous at the scheduled time to the exact second, characterize a mechanical civilization based on the application of the principles of science. In the sphere of production, efficiency involves attention to quality and to output per man-hour; in that of administration, impersonal decisions, perseverance in overcoming obstacles, a railway time-table on which the traveller can rely. To achieve it requires a considerable output of mental and physical energy. To certain classes in certain nations it is a fetish, to other sections of humanity a ridiculous fad.

The removal from key posts in colonial territories of a large number of persons who worship efficiency will have its effect on the way things are done in future in those territories. Will the result of their going be felt in the form of hardship? In a great many cases, probably not. If trains are not clean or punctual, surgical instruments not always sterilized, university qualifications not recognized as equivalent to those obtainable in Britain, this is a small price to pay for freedom and it may not even be felt as a price. But a point can come where the price of a decline in efficiency is generally felt even if the cause is not recognized. For one thing which ultimately depends upon efficiency is the level of incomes. Now, however much colonial peoples may question the other benefits which their rulers claim to have conferred upon them, they do not question the desirability of a money income; and if productive efficiency should decline to a point where incomes fall appreciably from even their present low level, this will be very widely felt as a hardship.

At the moment, in the newly-emancipated countries, production has very seriously declined. The major reason is not a decline in efficiency but sheer physical insecurity. The Viet-Namese and Indonesians can put the responsibility for this on the refusal of their former rulers to abdicate their position, but the Indians and Burmans cannot.

This brings one to the final question in debate: how far has emancipation resulted in – to put it as euphemistically as possible – a decrease in personal security, and how far is this to be regarded as a part of every man's right to be miserable in his own way? It is difficult to take up a position on this question which cannot be criticized as hypocritical. Who are we, who have reduced the cities of Western Germany to rubble, to hold up our hands in horror at communal massacres in India? The answer is, I think, that it is not a question of comparing the magnitude of crimes. All destruction, all slaughter, are deplorable, and any island, however small, in which destruction and slaughter are prevented is so much to the good. India, up to August, 1947, was such an island, and a large one – a single State possessing authority sufficient to prevent slaughter on a large scale. Now the Indian sub-continent is divided between two major States (with a number of minor ones) in extremely strained relations and not apparently possessing this authority. This is a net loss to the world, and it is hard to see who gains by it in India.

This Indian problem has its analogues elsewhere – the problem of a territory on which unity has been imposed by external force, where the inhabitants are united in the desire for independence but divided by interests just as strong, where the question 'Independence for whom?' is at the back of the constitutional demands of today in which each party is seeking to stake its claim for tomorrow. Outside India the problems of a plural society have been created by immigration fostered by the metropolitan powers, of Dutch in Indonesia, Chinese in Malaya, Jews in Palestine, Europeans and Indians in East Africa. In each case the immigrants have had an economic equipment superior to that of the indigenous people and have established themselves at a higher economic level. In each case the ruling power, after favouring the immigration, has felt itself bound to protect the interests of the indigenous population as the weaker party. In each case, with the exception of Indonesia, it has been driven to modify this policy under pressure from the immigrants. Disunity in Indonesia appears to be a matter of local rather than communal interests. In all the other cases communal claims are being pressed, and such voices as may be raised in favour of co-operation are barely heard. Even where there are no rivalries between communities, the question may arise whether the nationalists do represent a nation or merely a group drawn largely from a limited area in the colony for which they speak.

We cannot tell when, in each separate case, the moment will come for that transfer of power which is now recognized as both inevitable and logically necessary. We only know that it is much nearer than anyone would have dreamed ten years ago, and that whatever may by that time have been done to prepare for it will be short of the ideal aimed at by those – and they do exist – who seek to make colonial rule a means to the advancement of colonial peoples.

The task now is to lay such foundations as will give the colonies the best possible start when the time for transfer comes. On the economic side this involves a development policy which will result in a permanent increase in productivity, and this in turn involves the active interest of the people whose hands are going to do the work in putting the policy into effect. It involves the securing of goodwill, and it involves the training of many more persons both in manual skills and in the tasks of supervision and management. In all these directions the problem is to make up for the time lost during the era when paternalistic efficiency was the method and the justification of colonial rule. Nobody is to blame for not having foreseen the change in the climate of ideas; but many will be blamed in the not so distant future if the necessary adjustments to it are not made. Not the least of the difficulties to be overcome will be the conservatism of the individuals whose co-operation is sought – mistrust of new methods perhaps complicated by mistrust of those who advocate them. Any development which requires the individual action of millions of people entails endless patient persuasion – if the method of force is rejected.

On the political side, it is hoped that the co-operation of the leaders of local opinion in constructive plans will be more readily offered now that the weight accorded to them in the political organization has been increased. Yet it would be an illusion to imagine that this co-operation will be secured without unremitting tact and sympathy and much patience. Above all this patience will be needed in the colonies where there are communal divisions. We have seen the tragic consequences of letting these take their course. There may be circumstances where such divisions are irreconcilable, but where there is any hope of finding common ground it must surely be a major task of the governing power to try to bring the two sides together.

It is not sufficient to rejoice in the approach of the day of freedom; it is essential to realize how immense a task has to be done, and in how little time, to secure that the price of freedom shall not be too high.

10

How Small-scale Societies Change[1]

I originally intended to announce this address with the title
'Room for Manoeuvre', but then I was afraid that might be too
cryptic. All the same, the phrase does indicate my theme. I want
to suggest by it the way a social anthropologist looks at the
changes taking place in those parts of the world that have only
recently become interested in the application of science to the
control of their environment, in large-scale production and
trade, and in the development of industry and mechanical transport.

Some people think of social change as a phenomenon in itself,
to be studied separately from the analysis of social relationships
that is our main job. Some people talk about 'explanations of
social change' as if it was something curious that had to be
accounted for; as if one expected societies to stay permanently
the same and was surprised when they didn't. Some people
think that to have experienced little social change is to have had
no history. This attitude is very widespread in Africa, where
people are coming to resent very much the idea that nothing of
any importance happened to them before their continent was
invaded by strangers from the east and north. They resent the
idea that nothing can have happened because there are no written
records of what happened. But the fact is that many countries
which have historical records going back for millennia can also
be thought of as having experienced little change during most
of that time in comparison with what they have gone through
in the last two or three generations.

Along with the attainment of independence by so many African

[1] Presidential Address delivered to Section N (Sociology) on 28 Aug. 1964,
at the Southampton Meeting of the British Association; reprinted from *The
Advancement of Science*, XXI, 1964-5.

states there has come a great interest in Africa's past, and we learn more every day about the rise and fall of ancient empires – just the kind of thing we have learnt from records about ancient Asia – and about the migrations of peoples. But we don't learn very much about the social changes that accompanied these events. Of course we know that immense social changes must have taken place between the time when men first began to use tools – an event which may have happened in Africa – and the dawn of history. But one cannot hope ever to be able to trace those. We see that different African societies are organized in different ways, but we don't find that they themselves believe they have been through many changes; the older men at least consider that their world was created once for all in the form in which they first learnt to know it, that it has not changed and should not be changing as it now is.

When we speak of changes in society, we mean changes in the rules that govern social relationships – rules about the ownership and transmission of property, the right to exercise authority, the duty to co-operate with particular people in particular circumstances. In the main, these rules seem to have been little affected by the events that we know of in the pre-colonial history of Africa. We know that some peoples in their migrations took care to preserve their social structure as nearly unchanged as possible; for example, the Tiv in northern Nigeria, when they migrated, moved in such a way that the same land-owning groups were always neighbours. Conquest by invaders made conquered peoples liable to pay tribute, and the fall of empires relieved them of this burden, but these processes seem to have made very little difference to their conduct of everyday life. If we have found it is not true that Africa has no history, we must still agree that its history before the nineteenth century was not marked by striking changes in the general character of social relationships, and that if one contrasts the events of the last hundred years with those of preceding centuries, to speak of 'unchanging Africa' – or, correspondingly, of 'the unchanging East' – seems a pardonable exaggeration.

At any rate, this contrast has led a good many people to assume that social change is a peculiar phenomenon which students of society should be expected to *explain*. This really amounts to saying that we don't expect societies to change, although all of us in what is called the western world know by experience that the societies we live in are changing all the time.

What is the reason for this paradox? It arises in part from the very nature of the study of social anthropology. Our profession is concerned with the way small-scale societies work; this means that we look for the rules that are generally accepted and the social forces that support these rules. Since we are largely interested in the way societies very different from those of western Europe and North America can work, we sometimes try to picture what this was like before these societies had been radically transformed by influences from outside, as most of them have today. Also, there is a school of anthropology concerned almost entirely with the process by which, in different societies, children are moulded into the kind of person that the values of the society require. Both these approaches are better calculated to explain the persistence of traditional standards than the process of departure from them.

Most British social anthropologists now use as key terms in their discussion of social behaviour the concepts *status* and *role*, which were introduced into the subject by the American anthropologist Ralph Linton. When we speak of status we mean a person's position in his society, as it might be a point on a map, the sum total of his different relationships to other members of his society. To each of these relationships there is an appropriate role; that of father to son, chief to subject, judge to litigant, husband to wife, teacher to pupil, and their reciprocals. In every society the same individual is called upon at times to play many of these roles. One way of defining the structure of a society is to say that it consists in the configuration of role relationships.

One of my most distinguished colleagues, Professor Raymond Firth, has described this as a determinist way of looking at society. To him the metaphor of role suggests a part in a play, with lines laid down in advance from which the player cannot depart. Very few theatre enthusiasts would react to the word in that way. Quite apart from the fact that an actor may forget his lines and supply the lack by more or less inspired gagging, we all know that the smallest roles can be interpreted in half a dozen different ways and the major ones in a hundred. Indeed one writer, Professor Dorothy Emmet (1960), has expressly conceived social change as the cumulative effect of individuals' reinterpretation of their roles.

It is true that in societies which are not changing at a rapid rate most people's status is given, or, in technical language, ascribed. Some are born to high and some to low status, some to rule and some to serve; and if the accident of birth has assigned them to the lower ranks they are not likely to be able to get out of them. Again in technical terms, the opportunities of achieving higher status are not great; social mobility is little.

But this does not mean that to talk of the role appropriate to a given status implies that each man's destiny is fixed from the outset. Obviously no social anthropologist thinks so, but I am concerned to dispute the proposition that our way of talking logically implies it. Leaving aside the possibility of the reinterpretation of roles on a scale that would change the whole social structure, the roles themselves allow the players a freedom of choice which they use to further their personal interests. This is the freedom of manoeuvre that I want to talk about.

In any society some relationships are given and some are chosen. A very wide field of choice is open to the members of western society; within limits that are set by circumstances and not by prescribed rules, they can choose what work they will do and for whom, what interest groups they will join, what they will do with their property, what religious community they will attach themselves to. In the societies of simple technology that anthropologists have mainly studied, the field of choice is much narrower, but it is there.

In the first place, people can choose with whom they will ally themselves by marriage. In a society where a great number of roles are given through the fact of kinship and its obligations, the question with whom one will contract the additional obligations of affinity is of the utmost moment; this is why young people are not allowed to choose their mates without their parents' consent. In these societies, where polygamy is generally permitted, a marriage is the conclusion of an alliance, and by making a series of alliances in different directions a man can become influential as a negotiator between the people of his own and neighbouring communities. This is one way of building up prestige.

Then people have some freedom to choose where they will live. Even in those societies where the solidarity of the extended family is the ideal, one will find people who have attached themselves to a kinsman outside this group because they have more to hope from him in the way of protection or material help. In agricultural societies a man may choose not to live on the land where he has rights of ownership in virtue of descent, but to go elsewhere, again choosing the person on whom he will be dependent. In some societies there is no claim based on descent as such, but people choose between a number of localities in which they have kinsmen.

The institution of clientship, in which the poor and weak attach themselves as retainers to the rich and powerful, offers another possibility of exercising choice. Several anthropologists have recently studied this institution in East Africa. As they see it, the client may be driven to seek a powerful man's protection because he is an outcast from his own people; or the society may be so turbulent that a big man needs a private following to defend his rights and a little man cannot exist unless he is attached to a big man. But even in such circumstances, a client can advance his interests by finding favour with his lord, so that he is entrusted with authority and with secrets. And there are other societies where it is a matter of free choice whether to live one's life as an ordinary villager or to offer one's services to a chief; ambitious men of humble birth choose the latter for themselves or their sons, as a way of making their fortunes.

The men who can offer protection or material assistance to others use this advantage to build up a following and so increase their own power, particularly when there is a competition for leadership in view. A recent study of a people in Northern Nyasaland (Velsen 1964) shows how a man whose ambition it is to become the head of a village will do everything he can to persuade the junior members of his lineage to live in his village and not in those of other kinsmen – another illustration of the fact that there is room for manoeuvre even where there is supposedly a clear rule as to where people should live.

I have given these instances in order to correct an assumption that is too often made about peoples whose social structure has changed little over a long period of time. This assumption is closely connected, in logic if not in argument, with the idea that it is deterministic to talk of a social structure which allocates roles. It is the assumption that in societies based largely on ascribed status every person's life is mapped out for him at birth – an assumption that nobody would make about western society, though most students of western society find it useful to consider it in terms of statuses and roles. The kind of anthropology that concentrates on what psychologists call the learning process and sociologists that of socialization makes the same assumption, though for different reasons. Detailed studies are made by this school of the explicit transmission of culture – the ways in which children are taught the rules and values, as well as the technical skills, of the society they are growing up in – and also of ways of treating children that are taken for granted rather than deliberately taught to anyone, such as what is so primly called toilet training. When every factor in the moulding of the personality has been explained, the tendency is to assume that all the members of the society studied have been so strictly conditioned that they are unlikely ever to stray from the lines on which they have been set. As soon as this assumption is made, it becomes necessary to look for theories explaining why people ever behave otherwise than they have been trained to do. The theories that have been elaborated are concerned in general with items of behaviour rather than with social relationships.

At this point one should perhaps ask why people should recently have become so much interested in social change. Most of us have been taught history of some kind at school, and although I know it is possible to teach history without having much idea that one's own society has changed over the centuries, most English people are aware that our twentieth century world has been reached through a long series of events that both link us to and separate us from the ancient Britons. The anthropologists of the nineteenth century were so conscious of history that they spent most of their energy in trying to trace the imaginary course of pre-history. They invented events to explain the changes that they supposed must have happened, but they would have been astonished if anyone had told them that change in itself needs explanation.

The reason why people have begun asking for theories to explain change is not a philosophical but a historical one. It arises out of the events of the last century in the small-scale societies, and out of the preoccupations of the present day among the same societies.

The nineteenth-century anthropologists who thought they could trace a series of phases through which all societies had passed were in one sense on the right lines, though we seldom mention them now except to laugh at them. The series of imaginary transformations of society which they postulated no longer interest us. But isn't there a sense in which it is true that, in historical times, human societies have trodden very largely the same path? Robert Redfield had this in mind when he described his treatment of history as 'the story of a single career, that of the human race' (1953). When he said this he didn't imply, with the nineteenth-century writers, that mankind had grown from childhood to adulthood, or that societies could be ranged on a scale of moral or intellectual excellence. He simply had in mind that all through history the body of knowledge in the possession of mankind, and the application of that knowledge to the control of nature, has been steadily increasing. By means of a series of discoveries and inventions we have moved from the curse imposed on Adam – 'in the sweat of thy brow shalt thou eat bread' – to the affluent society. At least, part of the world has: the part in which social relationships have been reorganized in response to technical inventions, so as to exploit the possibilities of these to the full.

The question why inventions have been made at particular times and places is certainly one that calls for an explanatory theory. But this is not the question that is attracting attention today. What everyone is asking today concerns the response to the inventions of recent centuries of peoples to whom these inventions are alien. Inventions in communications made possible the era of colonial expansion. Other technical inventions made it possible to utilize the products of the tropics and the far east in all kinds of ways. People in these countries were encouraged, pressed, occasionally even forced, to grow for sale the raw materials for factories in Europe, or to provide the large labour force, concentrated in a few places, that is needed for the extraction of minerals. This made an upheaval in their accustomed way of life and in the social relationships by which it was ordered, an upheaval which many of them found uncongenial. But when these countries achieved independence, as so many of them have in the last few years under the leadership of men who have largely identified themselves with the new ways, their aim was not to return to the past, but to move faster in the direction of modernity than they had been able to do under colonial rule. In this they have the sympathy of the rest of the world, and particularly of the nations which already have a fully fledged machine civilization.

What really concerns both the new nations and their friends is not to know why or how societies change, but why they are not changing faster. In other words, the problem for policy-makers is to find explanations of conservatism, not explanations of change.

Is it profitable, I wonder, to approach this problem with the assumption that some explanation is needed for every occasion when a person departs by a hair's breadth from the behaviour that he was taught as a child? I do not exaggerate when I say that this *is* the approach of writers who tackle the question from the point of view of learning theory. When I talk about room for manoeuvre, I do so expressly in order to emphasize the view that details of behaviour are not so rigidly fixed, and that there are major fields of activity in which choice has always been open. I suggest that if the subject is approached in this way we shall find ourselves asking quite different questions and seeking quite different kinds of answer. We ask, then, what people may be expected to aim at in the choices that they make. Dr. Edmund Leach gave an answer to this question some ten years ago. In his view they 'seek to gain access to office, or the esteem of their fellows which may lead them to office' (1954). This is his way of spelling out the proposition that men seek power. I would agree with him that many men seek power, though I should not identify power with office. If power is the ability to control the actions of others it can be attained in other ways than by holding office: by possessing wealth, for example; this is a source of power in societies which have few or no recognized offices. Dr Leach might prefer to call this influence. Many men certainly seek wealth, but not necessarily as a means of power; it may be a means to physical comfort and enjoyment of various kinds. Most men seek the esteem of their fellows, but not necessarily, I think, for the sake of gaining power or office. The significance of the act of choice is that in making it a person may have to weigh the proportions in which either choice will gain him these different goods. They may well be incompatible on some occasions.

If one starts from this position one looks rather differently at the societies of simple technology which have been drawn into the world created by inventions made in other continents. One sees people who have always had open to them a certain area of free choice, but who now find themselves in a situation where the range of choice is much wider. There have always been choices which involved the disregard of obligations and, as a penalty for this, some loss of esteem. People who flout the laws of their society make that kind of choice, and there have been such people in all societies. Without incurring general contempt, a man may often think it worth while to make himself unpopular in a particular quarter; for example, if, as the authority over the disposal of the family herds, he lays out cattle to make an additional marriage for himself while a younger kinsman is unmarried. Anyone who has resources at his disposal often has to make up his mind whom he will assist, and this may very well entail making up his mind whom he will offend. It is by no means peculiar to machine civilizations that you can't please everyone.

I am suggesting, then, that whatever kind of society we are looking at, we see people facing alternative courses of action and choosing which they will follow. They may be choosing between equally legitimate alternatives; they may decide to break a rule or neglect an obligation and take the consequences, or hope to evade them. They make the choice in accordance with their calculation of relative advantages – one advantage being always that approval of one's neighbours which is gained by conforming to the rules that are generally accepted.

Every society, then, offers to its members opportunities of succeeding in life by various criteria of success, and the different criteria are, I would say, in essentials the same in all societies. It is the opportunities that are limited by the scale of the society and its technical possibilities, and what has happened to the small-scale societies in the last hundred years is an immense widening of the field of opportunity.

We do not have to consider in this context the causes of what the pundits call endogenous change, because it is a historical fact that the contemporary changes that we see in these societies have been stimulated from outside. External forces have brought to them technical inventions that were the culmination of centuries of history in Europe. They cannot fully profit from these inventions unless they are organized in an appropriate manner; that is, unless they quickly make the adjustments in social relationships that the older industrialized countries made at a much slower rate. Colonial rulers were interested in promoting some of these; they encouraged wage labour and the production of cash crops, and familiarized their subjects with a money economy, and they created much wider political and economic units than had ever existed before. Their road and rail systems, and their administrative organization, created the framework on which the present independent states are built, nearly all of them combining numbers of small-scale societies that were autonomous a century ago. This should be remembered when disunity within these new states is laid at their door and ascribed to their deliberate malevolence. The new independent leaders think their countries should be changing much faster; they set targets for economic growth, make large plans for capital investment, and seek, and receive, aid to these ends from the richer nations. Yet, as we have so often been reminded in the last few months, the gulf between rich and poor nations gets wider instead of narrowing. In part this is due to the inadequacy of the help given by the rich; but only in part. When capital is injected into the systems of the new states, productivity does not increase as it should in the calculations of economists; when farmers are told they could double their incomes if they changed their techniques, they don't seem to care; when women are told their children would be healthier if they boiled the water, they receive the news with sceptical indifference. Applied anthropology, once the study that claimed to have all the answers, is reduced to asking why.

This is the situation from which the demands for a theory of social change have sprung. In the old days we didn't call it social change; we just called it history and took it for granted. As I have suggested, many of the questions that are asked today about the nature of social change might be better described as questions about the nature of conservatism. The two kinds of question get inextricably mixed up, unless we realize that social change is the sum total of actions by people, and that at any given time some people are clinging to the manner of life in which they grew up while others are seizing the new opportunities that are offered them by the creation of new situations.

I would like again to emphasize the theme of manoeuvre and

choice. We are not dealing with habits that are hard to shake off, as is implied in so much writing on this subject, but with different preferences; those who prefer to play the old roles in the old way may well be the less imaginative, the people who don't see the advantages to be gained by entering into new relationships, but they may be people who, on the basis of rational calculation, have more to gain by sticking to traditional roles than by trying something else.

One obvious division in the small-scale societies is that between people whose ascribed status is high and people whose ascribed status is low. Naturally it is in the latter category that we first find men eager to try their luck in new worlds. Offered new roads to esteem, as scholars, or, much more commonly, as possessors of the new wealth, they go to school, or go to work at some distant place, more readily than would their age-mates who expect to succeed to positions of authority at home. And into this question there enters also the moral component of the role. I have stressed the view that esteem, or as some might prefer to call it, social approval, is one of the goods that men pursue. As Malinowski pointed out years ago, people do not perform irksome obligations out of mere force of habit or slavish adherence to custom; they play the roles appropriate to their status, as we should put it, because they are aware that obligations are reciprocal and that they cannot expect their own claims to be accepted unless they accept those of others (1926). But they are also subject to what Radcliffe-Brown called the diffuse sanction (1952) of public opinion, expressed in comments on the rightness or wrongness of typical actions, and statements of the reasons why they are right or wrong. They want to earn favourable comment, to be applauded for their interpretation of the role. Hence what they face when they undertake new roles is a crisis of conscience; new relationships are incompatible with pre-existing ones, *not* simply because they entail new kinds of action but because they necessitate the neglect of established obligations.

Hence it is of considerable significance whether the new relationships into which people enter take them away from the village environment. If their new roles are played before an audience all of whom have the same expectations – a city audience of workmates, foremen, employers, welfare officers and municipal authorities – they will learn them and stick to them. In the city the social pressures that act on each individual act in the main on the side of conformity to the rules of city life. The urban wage-earner soon learns the new routine of fixed working hours and the weekly pay packet. The conservatism of the countryside is not to be explained by the fact that all the bright boys leave as much as by the strong pressures that operate there in favour of conformity to tradition, simply because of the concentration there of the people whose expectations are those of traditional village life. It is easier to choose new roles in a context where you are not surrounded by old expectations.

Colonial rule created the new roles – the cash farmer, the wage earner, the civil servant, the politician, the nationalist leader. As long as all power was in the hands of the colonial bureaucracy, they defined the roles; they wrote the lines. A subsidiary part in the production was played by the missionaries who were responsible for most of the formal education; they injected the moral content into the new roles. But on the whole there was greater agreement between the values of church and state in colonial territories than there has been in the most highly industrialized independent ones.

The events of the last fifteen or twenty years have been marked by the rejection of the claim of Europeans to define the roles that Africans are to play. They have decided to put on a western-style production; that is to say they have committed themselves to 'modernization' in the economic and political fields. But the 'style' of the production is now to be African. It is often said, particularly in the field of politics, that it is to 'express the African personality'.

Before accepting this description I should like to look a little more closely at the political field. A good deal of attention has been given to political relationships since so many African and Asian countries attained independence from colonial rule. They embarked on their new careers with an outfit of parliamentary institutions provided by their former rulers, and usually desired by themselves. They were initiated into the use of the ballot box in their final years under colonial rule and thus launched, it was supposed, on a career of 'democracy'. Many of the people actually concerned in this operation thought of democracy in rather simple copy-book terms as 'freedom to choose the government', and consequently a party system offering the possibility of an alternative; or as 'government by discussion', therefore freedom to criticize those in authority.

As it has turned out, many of the new states have chosen not to allow organized opposition to the party in power, and in some of them there never was any effective organized opposition. Most of them suppress public criticism in one way or another, and most of them have taken a short line with individuals who were suspected of competing for power. This fact has caused concern in some quarters and sour satisfaction in others. It is popularly ascribed to the wickedness of leaders who are supposed to be bent on dictatorship. At a somewhat more sophisticated level it is explained, at any rate in Africa, in terms of traditional attitudes; African councils never divide into opposing parties, African tradition was to allow discussion before a decision was taken but no criticism afterwards. Explanations of this kind provide an answer to those critics who assume that only a two-party system is respectable, and the answer is in keeping with the ideology of the 'African personality', of something different about Africans which makes it inappropriate for them to imitate European institutions too closely. Such explanations are also popular with the school of thought that thinks of tradition as providing an outfit of habits, of stock responses among which the people try to find the appropriate one to deal with a new situation.

But this is not at all what is happening in the new states, whether in Africa or in Asia. It is true that they have had presented to them an outfit of political institutions that they might well not have developed in isolation. A large number of new political roles have been created, with a certain amount of instruction, in the form of a written constitution, as to how they should be played. But the instructions hardly do more than set the scene; the lines have not been written. In other words, this is an *open situation*; the actors can make what they like of it.

Now the contrast between the traditional political systems with hereditary rulers and the modern-style constitutions of the new states is precisely that in the old systems positions of authority are ascribed, while in the new ones they are achieved. Certainly, as Dr Leach has remarked, there was always competition for office, but the competition was open only to men of the right lineage. Now the field of competition is much wider; theoretically it is unlimited; this is the one of the implications of the word democracy that is most congenial to men with ambitions. New fields are open for the attainment and exercise of power, and new men enter them – people who see how to take advantage of a new situation.

They work out for themselves the means of attaining and holding power, using methods that are not narrowly defined by tradition but have been utilized from the beginning of time – rewards for services, revenge for injuries. Does anyone suppose that these principles don't operate in what we call democratic politics? The situation in which they are manoeuvring gives them a good deal more freedom than is characteristic of the older democracies, and they naturally take advantage of this. I mean that in most of the new states, the proportion of people who are capable of forming views about the problems that confront a modern government is so small that there is no material to make opposition parties out of, or a critical press. Of course there is discontent, but it is inarticulate discontent, of the kind that can be too easily answered by telling people they don't know what's good for them. This is just what the colonial rulers used to tell them, but again I am not suggesting that the new leaders are simply imitating their predecessors or, as it is sometimes called, borrowing from their culture.

I should seek the explanation neither in the imitation of a foreign culture nor in the attempt to apply traditional methods in a new situation. Rather I would say that here the new rulers have found themselves freed from traditional checks, because they do not have the relationship with the mass of the population that the traditional rulers had with their much smaller numbers of subjects. They have a new reason for disregarding criticism, because, unlike the older rulers, they do not see the world through the same eyes as their subjects, and they are occupied with affairs that leave them little time for that listening to personal grievances which was a large part of the traditional rulers' duty.

Clearly the struggle for power in the new African states is not going to be fought out in the more or less gentlemanly manner characteristic of countries with rival political parties. But this is not a matter of tradition or temperament; it is simply a matter of historical circumstances. In the newly independent states a number of roles have been vacated by European bureaucrats, and a number of others have been created by constitution-makers, both before and after independence. The public expectation of these roles is ill-defined; a few people expected them to be played strictly in accordance with the assumptions of older parliamentary democracies, a very much larger number had no particular expectations and didn't much care. Those who have filled the roles, whether they have sought them from a sense of mission or from less altruistic motives, have interpreted them in the manner that seemed to them best calculated to maintain their authority and maximize their power. The present social structure of these societies offers no effective challenge to this interpretation; as most students of politics recognize when they are thinking about it, phrases in constitutions have never by themselves been effective sanctions against abuse.

I have tried, with examples of people's conduct in different contexts, to argue that the social changes we are witnessing today are effected by social forces that have been in operation in all societies in all times – the manipulation of whatever areas of free choice there may be by people who are able to calculate where their advantage lies. When new opportunities present themselves, many people will hesitate to take risks with them, and some will perceive that their advantage would lie in the maintenance of the *status quo* if this were possible; they are the conservatives. Both types of person have always existed in all societies. What is peculiar about the changes of the present day in the non-western world is simply the breathless speed with which historical circumstances have extended the room for manoeuvre.

Tradition and Modernity
in the New Africa[1]

The intensive study of social change in Africa began with the founding of the International African Institute in 1926, and the policy followed at that time by the Rockefeller Foundation, which was generous in granting fellowships for the study of African affairs during the period between the wars. The subject has not lost its interest in these 40 years. On the contrary, it now appeals to specialists in a dozen different subjects, no longer only to anthropologists suspected of sentimentalizing about the African past. There is no need to spell out the reasons for this, above all in the city where the United Nations has its headquarters. But as one looks back over the development of the study, one is struck by the change in attitude of those who pursue it – something that seems almost like a complete *volte-face*. It might be an interesting subject for students of the sociology of knowledge.

In Britain the leading influence at the beginning of the story was that of Malinowski, who trained the first Fellows of the African Institute and supervised their research. In his own fieldwork, Malinowski had not been interested in social change. It is one of the many paradoxes of that remarkable man that, although the main lesson that he taught us was to look at society 'as a going concern', what he described in the Trobriand Islands was the 'going concern' *as it must have been* just before a colonial ruler began to interfere with it. Malinowski waged endless war against the crude ethnocentrism of missionaries and district officers, and his weapon was to insist that *everything* that had been done with the aim of improving native life and reforming native morals had in fact done nothing but disrupt the smooth

[1] Paper presented at a meeting of the Anthropology Division, New York Academy of Sciences, 25 Jan. 1965, and reprinted from its *Transactions*, Series II, **27,** February 1965.

workings of an almost ideal society. This attitude reflected his own disgust with machine civilization. He was supported up to a point by the missionary Edwin Smith. As a missionary Smith could not share Malinowski's wholly relativist, or even 'pro-savage', point of view; but he did urge an intelligent under-standing of African custom, and his influence was important in liberalizing missionary policy.

This climate of opinion influenced the fieldwork done between the wars. We all made ourselves the defenders of African custom against its critics, and against policies aimed at radical change. We all assumed that colonial rulers were both self-righteous and self-interested. But we did not at that time see the end of colonial rule as a possibility, so we contented ourselves with advocating the kind of policy that seemed likely to be least disruptive of African society: the recognition of traditional rulers and of customary law, and economic development based on peasant production rather than on wage-labour. This is the kind of policy that was favoured by Lord Lugard. The generation which sees us as old stick-in-the-muds might remember that this was the period when Norman Leys (1924) had just published his indictment of the ways in which labour was obtained for Kenya settlers; when the Belgians had decided that the recruitment of labour must be sharply curtailed if village life was not to be destroyed; when administrators in the catchment area of the Copper Belt were concerned at the number of villages where all the young men were away.

At that time the study of social change in Africa meant docu-menting the disruption of rural life. This was one of the major concerns of the missionaries, notably Edwin Smith and Diedrich Westermann, who supported the African Institute from its foundation. They were worried about the corruption of morals – the escape from the sanctions of village life to the *anomie* of the town, as we always thought of it in those days. They hoped that the research done under the auspices of the Institute would somehow show what could be done about this. We used to say that people should learn from the industrial revolution in Europe and so spare Africa its worst horrors. I am not sure what we meant by this.

This is not how people study social change today. Why? Is what I have been saying untrue? Or are we all such timeservers

that we change our views when power changes hands? The first
question must be answered by a negative; and I hope the second
may. But I think it is true that we now look differently at the
changes taking place in independent Africa, and this fact is not
unconnected with the impatience of Africa's new leaders for
ever more rapid change. We have been forced to open our eyes
to a wider range of facts. One new development is the dissatisfaction of all but the most fortunate of African farmers with the
life of the village. Another, of which nobody was aware 30 years
ago, is everything that is summed up in the cliché 'population
explosion' – the compelling reason why traditional techniques
of production are not good enough any more. It is still true that
many people suffer in periods of rapid social change, but it is
no longer practicable to protect them by slowing down the
process.

Hence the student of social change today finds himself more
interested in identifying the obstacles, in the hope of helping
to remove them, than in himself offering obstacles. We recognize
now that the problems that industrialization has brought with
it are the same all over the world, and are by no means solved
in any country. A closer look at African towns has shown us
that they are not anomic aggregations of population where
'anything goes'. There is more crime in a town than in a village
of a few hundred people, but towns are not populated entirely
by criminals; there are more couples who have not been formally
married, but not all the unions are merely promiscuous. One of
the most interesting studies made since the war is one directed
by Philip Mayer (1961) in a South African township, which
shows what strict rules of conduct can be imposed among urban
populations, where sometimes the specific institutions characteristic of the rural tradition are maintained.

We have learned to recognize that the new society which
African leaders are seeking to create must be built up by the
entry of the villager into new relationships, and that this process
must inevitably weaken the bonds that made the solidarity of the
self-sufficient village. The crucial problem today is how this new
solidarity is to be created. But difficult as this may be, we no longer
think it is any answer today to preserve the older solidarities
intact. In the field of social change the anthropologist today has
two main preoccupations. One is to understand the obstacles that

the social structure and cultural values of different societies may present to schemes for technical improvement; the work of Dr George Foster (1962) and Dr Ben Paul (1955) has provided us with many relevant illustrations. The other, which has been my major interest, is the interpretation of the political developments that have taken place in the newly independent countries.

It is common knowledge that the political leaders of the new states have not valued the representative constitutions with which they were launched on independence. They do not surrender their claims to being democratic, but they maintain that Africans have a different way of practising democracy. This argument links up easily with the idea of a unique African personality which the institutions of the new states must seek to express. The phrase is probably not to be taken too literally; it refers to a belief that there are common African values rather than to a theory that there is something common, and unique, in the structure of the African personality. I do not think this latter proposition would appeal to many psychologists; they would be quick to point out that the traditional cultures of Africa have been far too diverse to have moulded a common personality. The term used by French-speaking Africans, *négritude*, has no such implications. It seems to refer rather to a deliberate effort to re-establish an African tradition from which, they maintain, French education has cut them off. It has been applied mainly, and quite appropriately, to attitudes revealed in imaginative writing by Africans.

Is there really something peculiarly African which accounts for African departures from the ideal of democracy, at any rate as this is understood in western Europe and northern America? Some of the African apologists for the one-party state would say it does, and some anthropologists seem to be inclined to say so too. Both maintain that Africans, seeking a guide to the manipulation of political institutions that did not grow on African soil, find it in reproducing types of behaviour that characterized the village polity or the small-scale state of the earlier ages of African independence. The appeal to tradition to explain the suppression of opposition takes the form of asserting that according to African tradition, matters to be decided are freely discussed by the chief's council, but once a decision has been made it must not be criticized.

Do not such arguments really imply a kind of naïve racialism – the idea that there is something in the blood or bones of Africans that is alien to the procedures of counting votes for and against a proposition, or keeping the actions of a government under critical review? I should say this kind of thinking is more likely to be behind the arguments presented by Africans than the more sophisticated interpretations of contemporary Africa in terms of patterns of behaviour imposed by cultural conditioning.

I find both these interpretations unsatisfactory. The first does not need to be disproved to an audience of serious anthropologists. As to the second, there is not one common African culture, but a great number of different cultures, each characteristic of only a small section of the population of any of the new States. If the ministers and civil servants in these countries were really trying to reproduce the patterns of behaviour that each of them had learned in his home area, it might be impossible to develop any common norms of political behaviour at all.

But of course it is not in fact the intention of the African leaders to act in every situation in accordance with the traditions of the past; nor, in my opinion, are they so rigidly conditioned by the cultures of their village homes as to be unable to break away from the behaviour patterns they learned there. It is worth noting that the arguments from the traditions of the past are offered to people outside the ruling group as reasons why they should be content to remain outside. One does not find serious suggestions that the conduct of government business in general should be modelled on that of the pre-colonial states, still less of the 'village elders' in societies which were not organized as states.

We should surely bear in mind that the experience of the political leaders in the new African countries has been by no means confined to the villages where their fathers lived. Many have studied in other countries, and some have played political roles in long-established representative systems. I think particularly of those French-speaking African politicians whose background has been so fully described in Dr Ruth Schachter Morgenthau's brilliant book (1964). They have been members of French parties, of French representative assemblies, of French trade unions. Could it be seriously suggested that when they take up govern-mental responsibilities in Africa they shed all this experience and look for guidance to what they can remember of their childhood?

It is surely worth observing too that the suppression of opposition is not peculiar to Africa. A fair number of Africans have studied in Communist countries, though not many of these are at present politically prominent. But every African engaged in political life has heard of the 'Peoples' Democracies', and knows that they are based on the principle that we are told is laid down by African tradition – discussion before decision, no criticism afterwards. We, who have heard of them also, may wonder whether this neat formula, when offered by African leaders, does describe their own traditional procedures. If, and in so far as, it does, the reason is that traditional African rulers were not concerned with long-term policies of social and economic development, but with *ad hoc* decisions on day-to-day matters.

I think, however, that as we study political processes in African and other small-scale societies – and this has not yet become completely impossible – we begin to see the same divergence between ideal norms and actual behaviour that political scientists study in countries with constitutions. Given any recognized political status, on however small a scale, there will be competition for it, and the means used will be what the competitors can get away with. The smaller the scale of the society, the less is the opportunity for the use of organized force in the struggle, and the more easily, perhaps, can those who are dissatisfied with authority make their dissatisfaction felt. Yet I have been struck by R. F. Salisbury's (1964, pp. 225–40) discussion, recently published, of what he calls 'despotism' in the tiny polities of coastal New Britain. I deliberately take this example from outside Africa, because I think we are dealing not with cultural peculiarities of geographical areas but with the universals of life in society. The fact is that every study of a political system must ask how freedom is balanced against constraint, arbitrary action against respect for rules, the exercise of power against the checks on its abuse. After a period in which it was assumed that 'savage' rulers must all be bloodthirsty tyrants, there came a revulsion in which it was enough to find some checks on their power for us to call them democratic. Today, I hope, we can make more dispassionate analyses, which are not concerned with dividing sheep from goats. Then we ask where, in a modern state with its apparatus of power, should we look for the forces that keep power in check, and the answer may simply be that they do not exist in

countries where too large a proportion of the population is politically apathetic. If we accept this answer, we find our explanation
of contemporary African politics in a negative instead of a positive
factor.

Where then do we find that continuity that is somewhere in
every society, no matter how rapidly it is changing? Not, I
suggest, in any carry-over of old modes of action into new
situations, but in those situations that the new order has effectively
disturbed. In the political field, these are the situations where the
solidarity of long-established groups is stronger than the solidarity
of the new nation. Sometimes there are individuals with a vested
interest in this narrow solidarity; I mean, of course, where
traditional holders of power have maintained their position
during the colonial period and are still able to maintain it. This
power depends partly on the strength of tradition, but also partly
on the magnitude of the vested interests. In other words, the
hereditary rulers who play an important part on the contemporary
scene are those who have their own bureaucracies, composed
of considerable numbers of men who would have a great deal
to lose if their status depended directly on the government of a
unified state.

The best-known African example is the Kabaka of Buganda,
who successfully insisted on a degree of autonomy for his kingdom comparable to that of a unit of federation, prevented
the introduction of the name 'republic' for what would be so
called by any of his country's neighbours, and had to be made
president (though with very little power) of the non-republic
as the price of his agreement to its new constitution. It is usual
to blame the British administration for having entrenched the
Kabaka's power, though people who adopt this explanation do
not say what policy they consider would have been preferable.
This is an extreme case of the resistance of a political system
sanctioned by tradition against the encroachment of an authority
resting on popular choice – that of the elected government of all
Uganda. Although, in this particular situation, the awareness of
the Kabaka and his chiefs of what they would lose under a
unitary government is an important factor, the resistance of
Ganda in general to control of their affairs by people who are
not Ganda is not less significant. The feelings of the Ganda in
general are typical of the way in which the traditions of the past

affect the politics of today. It is true that there is no popular
demand for the recognition of opposition parties – not because
of any universally accepted African pattern of decision-making,
but because very few people think in terms of competing parties
at all. Where tradition makes itself felt is in these assertions of
small-scale patriotism that are condemned by the African leaders
under the name of 'tribalism'.

With few exceptions, opposition parties in the new African
states have been separatist, if not secessionist. They have not
offered alternative policies for their country as a whole, but have
pressed for the maximum autonomy and financial control
for the unit they represent, a unit defined by a common traditional
culture. If the rulers in power in the new African States hold that
this kind of opposition cannot be allowed, they can look to
precedents that owe nothing to African tradition. Their aim is to
build modern nations out of the congeries of traditionally distinct
units that each one contains. The national sentiment that they
wish to promote can grow only as a product of the constant
interaction that modern communications and a common language
make possible.

It is interesting that in the biggest of the African states, Nigeria,
these factors – a common language and the circulation of population – are present to a greater degree than in any of the others.
This is not the result of deliberate policies adopted by either the
British or their successors, but of the combination of a number of
chance factors. The Hausa of the North are traditionally mobile
people. Once they traded across the desert. Since communications
with the south were developed under British rule, they have
established their contacts in the south. The Ibo of the East were
the first to respond to the offer of European-type schooling, and
now they man the commercial offices of the north, and to a large
extent provide clerical staff for the Emirates as well. In recent
weeks it has seemed that internal discussions might split Nigeria,
or might have to be resolved by force. If this does not happen,
it will be because the mingling of tribes in the economic and
political systems has created the organic solidarity that Durkheim
wrote of – an interdependence too close to be disentangled. If
this is a just estimate of the situation in Nigeria, it shows how
new networks of relationship can overcome the divisive effects of
traditional solidarities.

As for those leaders of new nations who are afraid these divisive solidarities are too strong, what they are doing is to deny their existence and silence those who seek to express them. Whatever they may say, they are rejecting tradition, not returning to it.

12

Independent
Religious Movements
in Three Continents[1]

THE CASES TO BE DISCUSSED

It appears to be characteristic of a very large number of societies that from time to time movements arise in opposition to the established religious institutions, offering either new means of attaining the benefits offered by the established religion or new interpretations of its dogmas. The leaders of these movements often claim to have received direct revelation from supernatural sources, and for that reason are frequently called prophets, though this name is of wider application, embracing also such persons as the Hebrew prophets, whose chief function appears to have been that of moral criticism, and also the givers of oracles who have a recognized place in some established systems. There is no reason to suppose that the movements of this kind which appear among non-European peoples subject to European rule form a class by themselves, but, owing to the circumstances in which ethnographic information has been collected, the bulk of this refers to subject peoples, and among such peoples religious movements are largely concerned with the relations between subject and ruler.

Millenary cults, again, are sometimes treated as if they belonged to a class by themselves. I do not believe that a sharp distinction should be drawn between them and movements which attest religious autonomy without promising the immediate coming of the millennium, or between them and the cults which limit their activities to healing and the detection of witches. It is common for the prophets of millenary cults to offer these limited benefits in addition to the promise of the final regeneration of the world;

[1] Reprinted from *Comparative Studies in Society and History*, I, no. 2, Jan. 1959, The Hague.

sometimes they fall back on healing practices when the promise of the millennium is discredited; in any culture area millenary, healing and witchfinding cults will be found to have common elements of miracle, revelation and ritual.

I propose to discuss religious movements which have been recorded in three ethnographic areas – among the Indians of the American North-West, the peoples of the South Pacific, and the Bantu of southern and central Africa. In each of these regions a particular form of religious movement has been held to be typical: in the case of the American Indians this is the Ghost Dance, in that of the Melanesian peoples the 'cargo cults', and in that of the Bantu various reinterpretations of the Christian religion as presented by missionaries.

The Ghost Dance gained its widest popularity during the period of westward expansion when Indian tribes were being confined to reservations, cut off from their accustomed hunting grounds, and subjected to various kinds of pressure to induce them to settle as farmers on holdings allocated to them by the Indian Administration. The second and more famous Ghost Dance movement, which began in 1889, followed the extermination of the buffalo by white hunters, which reduced the tribes that had not been willing or able to take up agriculture to a state of complete dependence on government rations.

Wovoka, the prophet of this movement, promised his followers that a millennium was imminent in which 'the whole Indian race, living and dead, [would] be reunited upon a regenerated earth, to live a life of aboriginal happiness, forever free from death, disease and misery' (Mooney 1896, p. 654).

A volume describing all the recorded cargo cults was published by Worsley in 1957. There are records of such movements from 1892; their prevalence increased steadily during the inter-war period, and they attained their height at the end of the Second World War. After this they began to give way to movements in which the political content predominated. From the time of the 'Vailala madness' of 1919 all the movements have had the three themes of the return of the dead, the arrival of a miraculous cargo of trade goods, and the destruction of the European population.

The Koreri movement of the Schouten Islands (Netherlands New Guinea) resembled the Ghost Dance in that it was based on a myth of world renewal and took so much of its content from

Christianity that it almost deserves to be classed with the African syncretic religions. An admirably detailed account of this movement, based on the statements of participants, has been given by F. C. Kamma (1954).

The most obvious contrast between the cargo cults and the Ghost Dance is that, whereas the latter idealizes the world of past tradition, the millennium of the former consists essentially in the possession of the material wealth of the modern world. Both types of movement look to freedom from alien domination, but the cargo cult believers envisage a world where they will live as Europeans appear to them to do, enjoying wealth without working for it. The imitation of European behaviour (the District Commissioner writing in his office), organization (lining up after the manner of police or plantation labourers), and mechanical contrivances (wireless, rifles) is characteristic of the cargo cults. Some have gone beyond mere superficial imitation and have created functioning political organizations. The Koreri movement, which reached its climax under the Japanese occupation, developed into an organized resistance with political aims, though still relying on magical sources of strength. It opposed its own version of Christianity to that of the missions. The accounts which we have rarely make it possible to follow the process of transition, and the relation to it of the offer of political models by the European administrations. This is a subject that would repay further study; again there is a contrast with the American Indians, who were offered American-style political institutions on their reservations, but do not seem to have drawn from these any inspiration to develop organizations opposed to those of their rulers. Some cargo cults – notably Yali's among the Garia of New Guinea and the John Frum Movement on Tanna, New Hebrides – involve the express rejection of Christianity after an initial acceptance. In the Ghost Dance by contrast, as far as one can tell from the records, the identification of Wovoka with the messiah was held to be consistent with the doctrine received from missionaries.

In Africa the syncretic or separatist churches have been discussed at length by Sundkler (1948) in his *Bantu Prophets in South Africa* (for the Union) and by Balandier (1955) in his *Sociologie Actuelle de l'Afrique Noire* (for the Kongo on both sides of the Congo river). An instance in this area of the link between witch-finding movements and those of wider scope is the fact that the messiah of the new African religion described by Balandier, Simon Kimbangu by name, was in his brief period of activity the leader of a movement largely concerned with the detection of witches. The witch-finding movements which spread into Northern Rhodesia and Nyasaland have been described by Richards (1935) and Marwick (1950).

The movements in South Africa to which Sundkler has given the name of 'Zionist' are largely concerned with the detection of witches; those which he calls 'Ethiopian' are not millenary in character. The Kimbangist religion, or *Mission des Noirs*, is significant in that it expressly rejects Christianity and offers its own prophet as the counterpart for Africans of Moses for the Jews, Mahomet for the Arabs and Christ for white men. It has its own scriptures, in which a close parallel is drawn between the martyrdom of Kimbangu and that of Christ.

SURVEY OF THEORETICAL COMMENTS

Most theoretical discussions of these movements have considered together only those which have appeared in a single region, though the explanations offered are usually assumed to be of general application, and may well be so in fact. It is assumed that we agree on the question what are to be regarded as their essential distinguishing features. Mooney, who quoted parallels to the Ghost Dance from various other places and historical periods, describes them as 'religious abnormalisms based on hypnotism, trances and the messiah idea', and his parallel instances are marked in some cases by dancing as an element of ritual and in others by 'paroxysms of twitching and trembling' (1896, pp. 930–45). To Williams (1928) the paroxysms were the most significant feature of the Taro cult, which he regarded as pernicious for this reason alone. Stanner (1953) also attaches importance to 'the tendency to rapture and paroxysm', which he ascribes to 'the influences of psychic suggestibility, voluntary imitation, and the excitements of charismatic leadership with its new theorem of action'. The phenomena of dissociation mentioned in this paper are a feature which many of the movements discussed have in common with religious cults over a much wider field. Detailed study of these phenomena are of interest rather to the psychologist than to the anthropologist. To the latter it would be valuable to know much more precisely, in many of the cases recorded, what was their place in the movement, and, where they were not a feature of prescribed ritual, how and at what stage they became associated with the cult. It is perhaps worth recalling that, in the account given to Berndt (1952) of the cargo cult among the Kogu of the New Guinea Highlands, fits of trembling were said to have seized individuals before anyone appeared with a message from the spirits; while on Manus the seizures, as described by Mead (1956), were not passed on from one village to another by a process of imitation, as in the Vailala madness (Williams 1923), but began spontaneously after the arrival of the spirits had been reported.

We can at least reject Williams' interpretation of the hysterical symptoms as an outlet for the superfluous energy accumulated when labour was lightened by the introduction of steel axes, and a substitute for the excitements which disappeared with the suppression of head-hunting and pagan ritual; and the applied anthropologists of today would not follow him in recommending football as a therapeutic. Nevertheless, Berndt, though he does not seek to explain the shaking fits in this way, considers that the cargo cults as such reflect a development of interest in non-native activities which to him requires explanation; this he too finds in the suppression of indigenous outlets for energy and aggression.

Haddon (1917) remarked that 'an awakening of religious activity is a frequent characteristic of periods of social unrest'; and both he and Williams found in the earlier New Guinea movements evidence against the theory of the essential conservatism of native peoples. Williams likened the Taro cult to a biological mutation. One might ask in this connection what is to be regarded as a significant social change, and whether a new prescription for restoring a state of affairs consonant with traditional values should be so described.

Yet another explanation was offered by Williams when he ascribed the Vailala madness to mental indigestion caused by the presentation of Christianity to intellects not ripe for it.

Lowie, while following Haddon's view that social unrest is the predisposing factor for the appearance of new cults, is more specific. He contrasts the relatively slight extension of the Ghost Dance in 1870 with its widespread adoption in 1890, and after enumerating the hardships endured by the Indians in the later period, concludes: 'The intense emotional stress predisposing a people to yearn for deliverance from their ills is amply accounted for. In 1870 all these conditions were either lacking or much less acute, and the soil was therefore but indifferently prepared for the reception of a Messianic faith' (1936, p. 184). This comment raises the question *How much* dissatisfaction does it take to create a new religious movement – a question which has been discussed by Firth (1955) with reference to the cargo cults.

Elsewhere, however, Lowie argues, as do other American anthropologists, as if he considered that 'the sudden contact of an aboriginal and a Caucasian population' was enough in itself to produce the religious reaction. Discussion in terms of 'accultur-ation' and 'contra-acculturation' is peripheral to the interest of this paper. One might, however, mention the distinction drawn by Linton (1945) between 'nativistic' and 'non-nativistic' messianic movements, as recognizing the significant contrast between the backward-looking Ghost Dances and almost all other movements of this type.

Philleo Nash interprets 'nativistic' movements as a reaction to deprivation in the psychological sense, taking it for granted that such deprivations result from the situation created by conquest. He points out, however, that they may include not only the loss of satisfactions found in the traditional way of life but also failure to attain expectations aroused in the new situation. 'Skills were introduced which brought no rewards and values were introduced without appropriate skills for attaining them' (1955, p. 441). He considers that the significant predisposing factor is the failure of expectation and not the rejection of domination or of an alien culture as such. From an examination of the different forms which the Ghost Dance of 1870 took in different parts of a single reservation, he shows how its fantasy content was most aggressive among the sections which had suffered most at the hands of the whites.

During the period at the end of the Second World War when cargo cults were springing up in every part of New Guinea, various persons who were concerned with the interests of the New Guinea natives, whether as administrators or as anthropo-logists, sought an interpretation in terms of attitudes which need not seem to a European to be wholly absurd. The present writer summed up the view of this group in the phrase that the cargo cults were an expression of the natives' 'hopeless envy' of the material wealth of the European, and suggested that 'there is no way to meet them except the slow one of increasing the native's economic opportunities and giving him a reasonably devised education' (Mair 1948, p. 67).

Firth, recognizing that there is always and everywhere some incompatibility between wants and means of satisfaction, has considered more fully than other writers the question in what circumstances this will give rise to a movement in which, as he puts it, satisfaction is sought in an imaginative projection. 'Cargo cults', he writes, 'tend to arise as a resultant of several factors in operation together: a markedly uneven relation between a system of wants and means of their satisfaction; a very limited technical knowledge of how to improve conditions; specific blocks or barriers to that improvement by poverty of natural resources or opposed political interests' (1955, p. 130). They tend to arise in groups where the sense of communal responsibility is so strong that it is not felt to be adequate for individuals to be able to meet their wants by leaving the group. 'Education on the one hand', he says, 'and the provision of avenues of employment and political expression on the other would seem to be important alternatives to cargo-cult development' (1951b).

Stanner, in rejecting what he calls 'the hopeless envy theory', must be taken to reject also this elaboration of it. 'It is not easy', he remarks, 'to see increased "economic opportunities" or "reasonably devised" education as the simple panaceas'. This type of cult he considers as 'a redemptive act of faith by which what is "realized" as pragmatically difficult, or impossible, of attainment, is "seen" under charismatic leadership as becoming possible by the "grace" of the spirits or ancestors' (1953, pp. 68–71). This interpretation is in line with that of Keesing, who calls such movements an 'authoritarian way of salvation amid the uncertainties of modern experience' (1942, p. 77). Kamma (1954, p. 224) also objects to the idea of 'imaginary satisfaction', but he appears to think that this is offered as an explanation of myth in general.

Balandier (1955) in his massive study of the contemporary messianic movements in the French and Belgian Congo makes a number of comments, not all of which would be applicable to the earlier movements in North America or to the less sophisticated cults in the Pacific. He finds the treatment of the subject by 'Anglo-Saxon' anthropologists wholly inadequate, but after a careful reading one gets the impression that his strictures are directed mainly against those who regard these phenomena simply as examples of 'acculturation', on all fours with the 'borrowing' of a technique or a magical process from a neighbouring tribe (he does of course recognize that not all exponents of acculturation theory are as naïve as this). This would account for his insistence on the colonial situation as something *sui generis*; in the field of 'culture-contact' it certainly is, though it may well have points in common with other situations which have given rise to religious movements. It would also account for the emphasis placed upon his interpretation of these movements as a 'total reaction'.

Balandier advances a number of different reasons for the emergence of the *Mission des Noirs* and its offshoots: it represents an assertion of the African's ability to evolve a 'civilized' religion; it is a reaction in the field of fundamental beliefs, that in which the people feel themselves most gravely threatened (is this so?); it is a reaction in the only field where any resistance is practicable; it is a reaction in the field where defence against insecurity was traditionally sought. In his view, movements of opposition to the established order in primitive society have always taken a religious form. Finally – agreeing on this point with Sundkler – he remarks that the new social classes which colonial rule has called into existence have no other field than this in which to pursue their struggle for power (1955, pp. 477–9).

RELIGIOUS MOVEMENTS AND THE STRUGGLE FOR POWER

To the sociologist one of the most interesting aspects of these movements is their relationship with this struggle. It is recognized that established religions validate the political structure of the societies in which they are found. But new religions are by definition in opposition to the established religion; if the latter gave to its adherents all that they expected of it, new religions would not arise. In the field covered by this paper all the messianic religions are in some way concerned with the distribution of power. But their adherents belong to the section of the total society which has the least power, and in so far as we accept the explanation of these cults, or any of them, as offering a fantasy compensation for practical disappointments, we see in them not a reinforcement of political action but a substitute for it. Not all, however, have operated wholly on the plane of fantasy. How far, then, do the prophets under our examination provide their followers with opiates and how far with stimulants? The answer in any given case has naturally depended to some extent on ideas about the prospects of successful recourse to political action, including in this term rebellion as well as legally recognized forms of pressure, and the ideas held by the subject group will be modified by their experience.

Some American Indian prophets have led or inspired armed rebellion; some have supported war leaders, others have provoked aggression against the war leaders' will. Many have offered recipes for invulnerability, but the demand for these is just as likely to arise in response to fear of attack as from a desire to initiate aggression. Perhaps the attitudes are necessarily combined. At the time of the 1870 Ghost Dance the resistance to the whites which eventually led to the Modoc War of 1872 was encouraged by a shaman in what Nash calls 'the traditional association of shaman with factional leader', but the Ghost Dance prophet among the same people had no war-like message. Nash, however, correlates the abandonment of the Ghost Dance with the resort to direct aggression, and thus implies the hypothesis that the fantasy and the practical reaction are mutually exclusive.

Can this be asserted as a general proposition in the cases where events set in motion by a religious revival have culminated in an armed conflict? It might have the support of Balandier, who comments on one of his African examples that Utopian beliefs encourage passive rather than active resistance, and that they are accompanied by 'verbal' rather than 'direct' opposition, in which the weaker party can indulge at little cost in a violence that could not be translated into action without serious risk. He therefore discounts even explicit threats as simply verbal outlets for aggression; he draws attention to the fact that such threats, in the form, e.g., of formal curses, are held by Africans to be practically efficacious by themselves. Mooney, however, does not suggest that in 1890 the Sioux lost interest in the dance at the moment when they decided to leave their reservation and so incur the intervention of the troops, though they obviously could not hold five-day dances while on the march; and in their final ill-judged aggression the (defensive) magic of the Ghost Shirt was invoked.

But it is of course not possible to evaluate the content of these movements as if their aims were stated once for all, and remained fixed; nor is it possible to follow out the history of a wholly Utopian movement to its natural conclusion, whatever that may be, since these cults among subject peoples do not operate in sealed compartments but in the presence of the persons against whom their aggression, verbal, fantasy or other, is directed. People who are aware that their destruction is being promised to enthusiastic audiences are not often calm enough to derive reassurance from their own disbelief in miracles; knowing that they are objects of hostility, they demand the protection of the forces of the law. This commonly takes the form of attempts to crush the movement by the removal of its leaders, and arrests are often effected without meeting resistance. Where they are resisted, it is impossible to say what the progress of the movement would have been had there been no such intervention; perhaps it would not even be safe to say that movements which meet force with force must have been initially more disposed to resort to physical force than those which 'go underground' or peter out. It may be that the intervention itself changes the character of the movement, and matters of historical accident such as the nature of the weapons in the possession of the resisting group must affect the course of events.

The fact that the Ghost Dance ideology involves a complete rejection of the alien way of life places it in a different category from the other movements we are considering, in all of which the ideal world is conceived as in some way involving access to advantages associated with the dominant group. In the case of the Ghost Dance, the question of the relation between religion and politics can be reduced to the question of its relation to armed rebellion. Of the African religions, those of 'Ethiopian' type can be placed at the opposite pole; they are a direct means of pursuing power, though not in the formal political sphere, and they have their own internal political organization. The earlier New Guinea cults may be said to represent a transition stage in which the overt behaviour of the dominant group is imitated without the structure of relationships in which political power actually resides. One might put it that the symbols of power are grasped before the reality. The use of military titles, 'General' and 'Captain', is on record as far back as the 'German Wislin' of Saibai in 1892; Haddon thought this 'evidently a reminiscence of the old native word *kuiku-garka*, headman' (1917, p. 460). The prophet of the Taro cult in the Mambare valley in 1914 bade his followers go to their gardens in line, like police, and encouraged them with shouts which are obviously those of the parade-ground (Chinnery 1917, p. 453).

On other occasions an illiterate leader has established himself in an 'office' imitating that of the local official, or has appeared in public going through the motions of writing. The John Frum movement had its 'militia' commanded by captains and lieutenants, which 'exercised daily', its guard posts at which persons entering the village were questioned and the purpose of their journey entered in a register, and even its traffic regulation signs (Guiart 1952, p. 170).

Such actions may be viewed as part of a wider complex of imitation of European behaviour, and the whole complex might be interpreted either in terms of 'sympathetic magic' – behaving like the dominant group in the belief that this will raise the subjects to a status equal to theirs – or as a symbolic *assertion* that the subject group has in fact qualified for this status by adopting the behaviour appropriate to it. As the culture of the dominant group is more fully understood the grounds offered for this assertion become, by its standards, more valid. Balandier instances the importance attached by the *Mission des Noirs* to their possession of a corpus of scriptures as setting their adherents on an equality with those of the recognized great religions. Yet even in the *Mission des Noirs* we find what is perhaps an analogue of the cargo cults in the wearing of khaki as a 'uniform of hope and victory' (1955, p. 449).

Particularly interesting, though not surprising, is the part played in all these movements by the recognition of the technical superiority of the dominant culture. To the cargo cult adherents the consumer goods which they hope to possess and enjoy, and understand how to manipulate, and the types of capital goods that are familiar to them, are, as Balandier remarks, symbols of power even if not necessarily instruments of authority. These are associated with the ancestors, who are expected to use them for the benefit of their descendants, bringing the desired goods not by what we should call supernatural means but by steamship or aeroplane (sometime even lorry). To the same order of ideas belong the imitation wireless installations that have been set up in some cases, and perhaps too the 'heavenly telephone' used by one of the Bantu prophets described by Sundkler.

Although the cargo prophets seem to offer no more than a fantasy solution of their followers' problems and thus an alternative to political action, some of them have actually envisaged an armed struggle as a necessary means to the attainment of the cargo, and others have set up a temporal authority of their own which does more than imitate the behaviour of their rulers. It seems that in the period during which we have records of these movements there has been a steady development towards a more realistic type of organization. It is not always clear what has been the relation of practical modernization movements to cargo cults. In some cases the leaders of the former have been different men from the cargo prophets, who may have either used the latter's support or been opposed to them altogether; in one at least, a practical movement developed into a cargo cult, and this has a parallel in one of the Kongo religions.

The general impression derived from the literature on the Pacific cults is that, as in the case of the Ghost Dances, the destruction of the Europeans is expected to be the automatic concomitant of the return of the spirits and the arrival of the cargo. But in two cases of which we have full accounts, this is not so. The Kogu expected that they would themselves kill the Europeans when, on the arrival of the spirits, their dummy weapons were changed into real ones, and the Garia expected to have to fight the Europeans and not necessarily defeat them without losses. Even in the Vailala madness there were some reports that the cargo would include rifles.

In the Garia case we have also a feature which appears again in the *Amicaliste* movement among the Kongo; a primarily rational attempt by a native leader to raise the status or the material condition of his people is re-interpreted in mystical terms by his followers, and he is treated as a prophet without having himself made claims to supernatural inspiration. Yali, the Garia leader, was a discharged sergeant-major who was encouraged to further 'community development' by building a model village; the favour in which he was held by the missions and government contributed to the popular belief that he was supernaturally favoured also, and his followers assumed that his instructions were preparations for the millennium. André Matswa during his lifetime was concerned solely with the rational political demand for citizen status for Africans; after his arrest for subversive activities the popular imagination made of him a messiah.

In the African movements one may again see different types of connection between religion and politics. The founding of a new sect may be a means of asserting the autonomy of a tribal group *vis-à-vis* its African neighbours, without reference to its relations to the European authorities. A religious organization may become a pressure group making claims on the basis of the ethical assumptions of the Christian faith which is ostensibly common to rulers and ruled. It may, as Balandier suggests, be deliberately made a cloak for a political movement, or immediate political aims may be interpreted in millenary terms by adherents too unsophisticated to conceive them otherwise. It may lay foundations for political unity by combining social groups which in the past had no common ritual.

In the case of the South African separatist churches Sundkler has taken the first step in the analysis of the political and religious elements by distinguishing between the 'chief-type' leader associated with the Ethiopians and the 'prophet-type' leader associated with the Zionists. He also notes that it is the Ethiopian churches which aim at obtaining a fuller share for their members in the European world, while the Zionists, though claiming to heal sickness by virtue of a more powerful spiritual force than that commanded by the old-style diviners, are little interested in political advancement or the improvement of African status. The difference is of course correlated with the fact that the Ethiopian churches are mainly urban and the Zionists largely rural. The importance for either type of the apocalyptic message is here reduced to almost nothing; occasionally a new leader wins a following by announcing an imminent judgment at which only his adherents will be saved, but we do not find large bodies of people seeking a way out of their discontents in fantasy constructions.

Sundkler has studied these movements largely from the point of view of the personality and social status of the leaders. He remarks that in South Africa the religious field is the only one in which there is any opportunity for the ambitious African to exercise leadership, and also that the pattern of kingship characteristic of Zulu culture determines the way in which this is exercised. Leaders of Ethiopian churches have some of the traditional functions of chiefs, including the settlement of disputes; they are expected to be the spokesmen and champions of their followers in relation to the government; they sometimes claim, and are sometimes expected, to hold their position for life and pass it to their sons. Students of social structure might add that the creation of churches with membership limited to a single tribe or smaller unit may correspond to a desire to express the autonomy of the group through the only available form of organization; though of course there is no church extending its authority through a *whole* tribe. At the time when Sundkler wrote, Ethiopian churches had accommodated themselves to the South African situation to the extent of valuing the advantages to be derived from recognition by government and so of refraining from making demands of a type that might bring them into disfavour.

Matswa, as an example of the politician made a prophet by his followers, has already been mentioned. It remains to discuss the political aspects of the *Mission des Noirs*. This neither has overt political aims nor does it offer a means of hastening the millennium. It simply asserts the promise of an eventual second coming at which the African leader will be the king. It appears, however, that before the Kimbangist religion had been systematized by Mpadi, its adherents for several years expected the new kingdom to arrive every Christmas, and that on one occasion it was believed that on New Year's Day a flood would engulf all Ba-Kongo who had been hostile to the movement.

The organization of the *Mission des Noirs*, however, is almost as much political as religious. It is modelled on that of the Salvation Army, itself a church of military type. According to Balandier, it is tending to arrogate to itself all the basic social functions, religious, political, and in a very embryonic way, military and police. Further, it has political significance not in virtue of any direct opposition to Belgian authority but because it appeals to all the Kongo tribes whether in French or Belgian territory. This it is enabled to do by its doctrine, taken from Christianity, of a universal god transcending the divisions which are emphasized by the ancestor cult.

The chronological relationship of the movements in the three regions under discussion is not of very great significance. As it happens, the first Koreri movement of which we have knowledge preceded the Ghost Dance, and this in turn preceded the earliest recorded instances from Africa and Eastern New Guinea. The first independent African church and the first recorded cargo cult are almost contemporaneous. The syncretic religions described by Balandier are the most recent in origin, but they exist side by side with new secessions in the Union and new cargo cults in the Pacific. But one can relate the characteristics of the different types of movement to an evolution in the attitudes of subject peoples towards their rulers and towards the civilization of the latter. One can trace this in two ways: by examining the nature of the millennium as it is represented at different times and by asking what happened to the cults in which millenary promises are specific. Under the first heading we have to consider not only the way in which the ideal world is pictured, but the way in which it is expected to come into existence and the explanations that are offered for the differences between the world as it is and as it ought to be. Neither aspect of the cult ideology is, of course, open to the free play of the prophets' fantasy. The ideal world must be what most people desire, and the explanation must be in line with current explanations of misfortune and disappointments. It seems that before the appearance of a specific millenary prophecy there must be in existence a generally accepted myth to which the prophet may appeal. Firth mentions that on Tikopia, which has never had a cargo cult, rumours of a world cataclysm and of a promised cargo circulated while he was there. He concludes that there can be 'a cargo cult type of behaviour' without a cult. Surely this is far too narrow a category. His instances illustrate the much more general proposition that I have just referred to, which might be put in the form that in any society there will be found to exist stereotyped expectations, corresponding no doubt to certain basic hopes and fears, which can be activated either when the hopes and fears become pressing or when actual events conforming to some part of them occur.

The myth of world renewal characteristic of the Ghost Dance is one of the best known: a catastrophe will destroy the existing world and all those in it who have not deserved to survive, and a new more perfect world will take its place, in which living and dead will be united and all the ills of real experience will be eliminated. This is common to so many mythologies –including the Christian – that its absence is of more note than its occurrence. It does not appear, however, to have been characteristic of New Guinea peoples, with the one recorded exception of the Koreri myth on the Schouten Islands.

What is interesting for our purposes is the way in which the perfect world is envisaged by subject peoples, experiencing at the same time forced changes in their own way of life and contact with another which claims superiority and both offers and denies new opportunities.

There are several records of the messages of American Indian prophets. Some were recorded by Europeans who were present when they were delivered, some written down by themselves. That received by the Delaware prophet of 1763 and conveyed by Pontiac to a gathering of Algonquin tribes was taken down by a French priest. It appears to have been uncompromising in its rejection of the English, though more tolerant to the French; though even they were not to be imitated. 'Before those whom you call your brothers [the French] had arrived, did not your bow and arrow maintain you? You needed neither gun, powder, nor any other object. . . . When I [the Great Spirit] saw you inclined to evil I removed the animals into the depths of the forest that you might depend on your brothers for your necessities, for your clothing. Again become good and do my will and I will send animals for your sustenance' (Mooney 1896, p. 665). As regards 'those who come to trouble your possessions' – the English – the message is explicit: 'Drive them away; wage war against them; they are my enemies; send them back to the lands I have made for them'.

Smohalla's views were recorded by MacMurray, an emissary of the United States army who spent a year on the Upper Columbia enquiring into Indian grievances. MacMurray's unpublished manuscript is partly digested and partly quoted by Mooney. In Mooney's summary, Smohalla told his people that 'their present miserable condition was due to their having abandoned their own religion and violated the laws of nature and the precepts of their ancestors'. To him the settlement of Indians

on agricultural holdings was itself a violation of these laws of the
earth mother, and competition for control of land (hunting
grounds and fisheries) was the root of all evil since it led to fighting.
God had ordained that all land should be held in common.
Mooney's information from this and other sources does not
ascribe to Smohalla any explicit prophecy of the destruction of the
white man, though MacMurray wrote that at the same period
'some of the wilder Indians to the north have more truculent
ideas as to the final cataclysm which is to overturn the mountains
and bring back the halcyon days of the long past. As the whites and
others came only within the lifetime of the fathers of these
Indians, they are not to be included in the benefits of the resur-
rection, but are to be turned over with all that the white man's
civilization has put upon the present surface of the land' (Mooney
1896, p. 723).

Wovoka, the prophet of the 1890 Ghost Dance, delivered his
message to a delegation from the Cheyenne and Arapaho tribes
who came to learn his doctrine, and it was taken down by one
of them – according to Mooney, from dictation – at the time.
Here too the prophet himself is not on record as foretelling the
elimination of the white man. The essence of his message is:
'Jesus is now upon the earth. He appears like a cloud. The dead
are all alive again. I do not know when they will be here; maybe
this fall or in the spring. When the time comes there will be no
more sickness and everyone will be young again. Do not refuse
to work for the whites and do not make any trouble with them
until you leave them. When the earth shakes [at the coming of the
new world] do not be afraid. It will not hurt you' (Mooney
1896, p. 178).

Naturally the message was developed by the apostles, and it
seems to have taken divergent forms, a few holding that in the
ideal world all races would live peacefully side by side – though
separated – others that the whites would be destroyed by fire or
flood, or, as in the case of the Pawnee, by a great wind.

In all these cases the ideal world represents a complete return to
the past, a rejection even of those material objects which have
aroused the envy of most peoples of simpler technology, and
of course of many Indians also. The Ghost Dance ideology is
generally regarded as representing a fantasy compensation for the
loss of all hope in the real world, and it was certainly most popular

among the tribes which had been reduced by the extermination of the buffalo to the condition of helpless dependents of the United States government, and least so among those which were obtaining a reasonably satisfactory living as farmers.

The characteristic feature of the cargo cults, in contrast, is an intense interest in the material possessions of the dominant group. Although, as has been mentioned, the cult activities reflect an equal interest in the rulers' ability to exercise power, it is the goods that play the central part in the ideology. In this case the very roots of the myth seem to lie in the 'colonial situation', since its theme is the misappropriation by Europeans of goods destined for the natives, goods of which they had no knowledge until Europeans appeared in possession of them. The cases quoted by Haddon indicate that it was in existence from a relatively early period of European activity in New Guinea. If we ask why, in this case, European possessions excited cupidity instead of the aversion to everything European manifested in the Ghost Dance, the answer may be that the New Guinea natives were not forcibly cut off, as were the Indian tribes, from their accustomed way of life. They were not moved from their traditional homes to a different environment, nor deprived of their traditional mode of subsistence. Thus their desire for European goods was not countered by that longing for a lost way of life which gained the upper hand among those Indians who adopted the Ghost Dance, and who, of course, up to that time had not rejected foreign goods.

The longing for reunion with the dead, which is a universal human experience, does not seem to have given rise to a myth in New Guinea apart from the Koreri story. But the belief that they remain in touch with the living is, of course, characteristic of New Guinea as of most other societies; and it might be regarded as a 'natural' reaction of people living in what they suppose to be a self-contained world to interpret the appearance of human beings unlike any seen before in terms of a return of the dead. It is on record that members of exploring parties have been welcomed with great emotion as returning ancestors. Nor is there anything logically outrageous in the assumption that the new goods, some of which are in fact usually given as presents to smooth the explorers' path, have been brought expressly for the benefit of their descendants. It is of interest to note that an identical reaction was met with among Amerindians in British Guiana.

By the time experience has proved this explanation to be false, the hopes built on it have become too dear to be abandoned, and there now comes into existence the myth of the gift from the ancestors diverted from its rightful owners by the Europeans. This is a simpler analogue of the belief in a false version of Christianity propagated by the missions which has gained so much ground in Africa; and indeed the theme of deception by the missions is also current in New Guinea, though it there takes a cruder form than in Africa, being concerned primarily with cargo and not with the brotherhood of all the children of God. Once a myth of this kind is current, it is easy to see how events are interpreted in the terms which it gives; Firth's example from the Tikopia, who had had no such belief on his first visit twenty-five years earlier, is interesting here.

Lawrence's (1954) reconstruction of the history of Garia attitudes towards missions and cargo traces a sequence which may well be typical. Believing as they did, he tells us, that their own gods could be constrained by the appropriate actions to give them what they desired, the Garia saw the rites of Christianity as a means of constraining a more powerful god, and readily abandoned the 'heathen practices' which missionaries condemned. Since missionaries have frequently urged their converts to destroy their 'idols', it is not surprising if the latter sometimes actually do so; nor is the association of a large-scale public exposition and destruction of magical objects with a cargo cult as remarkable as Williams thought it, if we see this as symbolizing a transfer of allegiance to the source of greater benefits. In the case of the Garia a mass baptism held in 1937 was preceded by such a public demonstration of the rejection of idols, and this seems to have been the model imitated by Yali's followers. In other parts of the world, too, this is a recognized symbol of conversion, of the making of a new choice or the rejection of some accustomed practice; it has been mentioned as an element of the Kimbangist religion, and is necessarily prominent in the cults which are primarily directed against witchcraft.

Among the more impatient Garia converts the idea became current that, just as some of them had secret prayers which gave them compelling power over different deities, so the missionaries had a secret prayer which they had not revealed; in fact they had deceived the people with false promises. At this stage arises the search for a direct means of communicating with the sources of cargo or a more effective way of coercing them. The prophets who attached themselves to Yali put their faith in a traditional god, but Yali himself was on good terms with the local missionaries at first. When he turned against them, he – unlike the more sophisticated African prophets – reverted to the traditional god instead of developing his own version of Christianity; it has been pointed out that Yali is one of the few prophets of any note who have been illiterate.

The New Guinea millennium, then, is seen in terms primarily of the possession of material goods but also of an enhancement of status for the subject group. Several myths refer specifically to the latter point. The returning dead are expected to be white-skinned and the living natives to become so; or the world is to be literally turned upside down, and black become white and white black; in the Koreri movement there were incidents when the reversal of roles of the natives and Indonesian officials was actually effected (Kamma 1954, p. 167). The John Frum millennium combines fantasy and practical aspirations in an engaging way. John Frum will supply all material needs, so that work will be unnecessary; he will also provide schools giving a better education than that of the missions and pay salaries to chiefs and teachers (Guiart 1952, p. 166).

On the millennium in Africa the most succinct comment is that there is none. The African churches represent a stage of development beyond that at which an immediate solution of all difficulties is expected. They may be said to embody the answer to the question what happens to millenary movements when they fail, as they must, to come up to expectations.

MORAL TEACHING OF MILLENARY PROPHETS

Before going on to this point, however, we should consider some other themes which will be found to be common to most of the movements.

In the first place, the coming of the millennium is rarely to be brought about by ritual alone. A moral code is often part of the prophet's teaching; and there is often, as well as the rejection of certain kinds of conduct which this implies, a symbolic rejection involving the destruction or abandonment of some material objects. These two features can be seen as expressing the idea that obstacles to the coming of the millennium have to be removed. The first, however, taken by itself, demonstrates the concern of the prophets with the ills of everyday life, such as sickness and tension within small groups, which they share with the humbler healers and diviners.

In the case of the American Indian prophets the moral message is part of a consistent whole; the believer must please God by conduct as well as ritual, and it is often asserted that existing misfortunes are a punishment for breaches of his laws. This theme has no place in the New Guinea cults, emphasizing as they do coercion rather than placation in their relation to their gods. Yet New Guinea prophets are on record as condemning such acts as theft, adultery and quarrelling. The African religions tend to emphasize traditional practices, such as polygyny and the levirate, which are not permitted by the missions.

Among the cases mentioned by Mooney, the Delaware prophet of 1762 was instructed by the Master of Life to tell his followers: 'Let them drink but one draught, or two at most, in one day. Let them have but one wife, and discontinue running after other people's wives and daughters. Let them not fight one another. Let them not sing the medicine song' (Mooney 1896, p. 665). The Shawnee prophet of 1805 began his 'earnest exhortation' by denouncing the 'witchcraft practices and medicine juggleries of the tribe'. He threatened torments after death to those who drank 'the firewater of the whites'. 'The young must cherish and respect the aged and infirm. All property must be in common' (Mooney, p. 672). The Kickapoo prophet of 1827 told his followers 'to throw away their medicine bags and not to steal, not to tell lies, not to murder and to burn their medicine bags' (Mooney, p. 695). Wovoka, the initiator of the 1890 Ghost Dance, was told by God to 'tell his people they must be good and love one another, have no quarrelling and live in peace with the whites, that they must work, and not lie or steal; that they must put away all the old practices that savoured of war' (Mooney, p. 772). How one longs to have been able to investigate such a statement at the time. Was Wovoka really a pacifist, or was he merely urging the Indians to keep the peace among themselves? It does seem to be clear that he told them to cease from internal war.

In New Guinea we learn that the prophet of the Kekesi cult

forbade his followers to carry weapons in the gardens, and (as translated by Chinnery) said: 'The people are to hear and obey the government. The people are to observe the moral code of the tribe. Food is to be properly cultivated, and no wastage is desired by me.' Later he announced that Kekesi was angry with a man who had stolen his brother's wife (Chinnery 1917, pp. 452-3). The Taro cult prophet told Williams that God had given him commandments 'against "swearing" [i.e. abuse, wrangling], theft, adultery and anger, and two positive injunctions – to be like the missionaries and like the white men' (Williams 1928, p. 75). In the Vailala madness various people claimed to have received direct ethical instructions from God. According to Williams, 'Thou shalt not steal, commit adultery, nor break the Sabbath, are the three commandments most frequently heard' (Williams 1923, p. 25). Mead (1956) lays great emphasis on Paliau's injunction to refrain from quarrelling or giving support to a kinsman involved in a quarrel; she interprets this as part of a rational policy which he adopted after repudiating the local cult. Such commands, bearing as they do on the unity of the group, have a dual significance; they relate to the ideal of internal peace which is part of every tradition, and also to the need for union in the face of external pressure.

Sundkler mentions various rules of dress and behaviour which serve to identify the members of different churches, but does not indicate that their leaders appeal for any kind of moral reform. He notes, of course, as does Balandier, their insistence that polygamy is not contrary to religious teaching. In the latter's view this is prompted not only by practical reasons, but also by a nationalist determination to maintain a distinctive institution which the foreign rulers have treated with contempt.

Examples comparable with those from the other two regions can be found elsewhere in African material. Gluckman has noted in the Mau Mau movement, along with insistence on the sexual freedom permitted by Kikuyu tradition, a puritanical attitude to indulgences learnt from Europeans which condemns smoking and prostitution with equal severity. I might also quote the commands given in a recent Ashanti witch-finding cult: 'Do not commit adultery; do not swear against thy neighbours; do not steal; do not harbour evil thoughts against anyone (Ward 1950, p. 53).

We can perhaps draw from these injunctions the conclusion that millenary dreams, concerned as they all are, in one way or another, with rejection of an inferior status, never entirely displace the everyday wish for peace and good will within the small community, to be attained by respect for the rights of others and by eliminating causes of quarrelling such as drink, and the dreaded concomitant of quarrels, sorcery.

OTHER CHARACTERISTIC THEMES

In addition to their strictures against socially disruptive behaviour, the prophets' teaching often involves the renunciation or destruction of specified material objects, either because they are conceived as obstructing the coming of the millennium or because they symbolize something which is in contradiction to the new doctrine. The destruction of symbols of a religion which is abandoned of course has an obvious significance, as has that of objects used in sorcery. In South Africa the Zionist churches reject European medicine, claiming that they possess the only true means of healing. The Ghost Dance adherents 'discarded everything they could which was made by white men' – though they had to make their invulnerable shirts of cotton cloth. The John Frum movement is unique in that it required its followers to get rid of all European coinage; two reasons were given – that when there was no more money the traders would have to leave the island, and that John Frum would supply a new currency. The 'Noise' which preceded the Paliau movement on Manus called for the destruction of all native-made goods, but in the excitement which broke out when it was reported that the magical ship had actually arrived, it appears that people exceeded their instructions and also threw away some of the possessions that they had acquired from the American troops. The taboos imposed by Angganitha, the latest Koreri prophet, do not seem to have had any symbolic meaning of this type.

Another recurrent theme is that of a human rescue by the action of Europeans of another nationality than that of the current rulers; this of course can only arise if there are circumstances which make the idea plausible. I suggest that there is a very early example in the 'German Wislin', with its suggestion that help will come from the other European nation installed in New Guinea, and that it is paralleled by those cargo cults which include the return of the Americans in their myth. In Africa, again, the followers of Matswa believed that the German advance in Europe in 1940 was a prelude to his 'vindication' and establishment as their king. One may associate these ideas with the notion that is so widely encountered in Africa, and no doubt elsewhere as well, that, however dissatisfied people may be with those in immediate authority over them, there is always, at some higher level, a just ruler who 'loves us', and, if he knew what was going on, would intervene to put things right. And this again has something in common with the belief that new and strange objects of wealth must be destined for the people among whom they appear, and must be intended as a gift for them from some being who is interested in their welfare.

The idea that the prophet himself has returned from the dead, and has originally received his message not by the recognized process of possession but by direct speech with its supernatural giver, is also widespread enough to deserve mention.

Something should be said too about the very common belief that when the millennium is at hand there is no need to go on with normal economic activities. How far is that the 'act of faith' to which Stanner refers, involving a practical expression of confidence in the benevolence of the spirits? Occasionally, though not always, the dogma is that all consumable goods must be used up or got rid of before the millennium can arrive, but this does not by any means always involve sacrificing the enjoyment to be derived from them. In some cargo cults the people threw their pigs into rivers, but in others they ate them in a succession of feasts. This could not be described as a hard way to salvation.

If the data from the three regions are compared, the theme of guilt – of having brought about one's own misfortunes – seems to be explicit only among the American Indians, while the theme of deception – of having been misled as to the means of commanding supernatural power – is absent there. No doubt the difference can be correlated with the Indian lack of interest in any advantage to be gained from participation in European culture. The theme of peace and good-will – for I suggest that this is the essence of the moral teaching of these religions wherever it is recorded – is common to the millenary movements, but in Africa is replaced by a nationalist insistence on rules of conduct which differentiate the subject from the dominant group. The theme of symbolic rejection is found in all three regions, though in the case of the *Mission des Noirs* Balandier emphasizes that it rejects material symbols in favour of a more abstract kind (Balandier 1955, p. 451).

What is the fate of religious movements which hold out specific promises that they cannot in the nature of things make good? In the majority of cases they are not put to the test, since their activities are usually suppressed by authorities which are either afraid of subversion or concerned at the consequences of the destruction of property or cessation of work, or both. There is thus usually open the explanation that the actions necessary to produce the millennium were obstructed by *force majeure*. But this is not always enough to maintain the faith of the believers. I suggest that there are two main reasons for this. One is that after a period of extravagant collective expectations people lower their sights and return to preoccupation with personal problems of sickness or failure in their own enterprises; the other that, as their understanding of their situation increases, they see it in more realistic terms, and look to solutions in which supernatural intervention plays a smaller part or no part at all.

It is important for the first type of development that the cults usually combine healing and sometimes also the detection of sorcerers and witches with the preparations for the millennium. Hence there is a way out for the prophet in reversion to traditional practice in this field. For example, Doctor George, the prophet of the 1870 Ghost Dance in the Klamath Reservation, had a long and successful career as a shaman after the failure of his specific for invulnerability brought his Ghost Dance message into disrepute. What is more interesting in this case, however, is the character of the new doctrines which took the place of the Ghost Dance among the same people. Nash's reference (1955, pp. 424ff.) to the shift in religious interest 'from a world event to the self' expresses, I think, the point made in the preceding paragraph. The first successor to the Ghost Dance was the Earthlodge cult. This too was concerned with the return of the dead, but without reference to any specific event such as the earthquake associated with the Ghost Dance. The Earthlodge cult gradually merged in the Dream Dance, in which all kinds of individuals had dreams giving them personal instructions, and this in turn into shamanism of more or less traditional type.

The 1890 Ghost Dance, according to Mooney, continued to be performed for a few years, but without the conviction that the performance would immediately bring the ideal world into being; it had become an expression of hope for an indefinite future.

The information collected by Kamma shows that the Koreri leaders found various lines of retreat. One took service with the Japanese, and was beheaded by them when they guessed that he was planning to go over to the Americans. Another withdrew into the interior and there organized the revival of the traditional ceremonial dances. Their followers returned to the mission churches, from whose teaching they did not consider that they had ever departed.

In Australian New Guinea we have seen the appearance of leaders offering practical betterment schemes, and organizations directed towards the autonomous control of local affairs. The relation of these to the cargo cults is by no means clear from available descriptions, but Yali's case shows that actions which are advocated on practical grounds may be given a mystical interpretation. However, one might guess that, as the leaders of any community develop a better understanding of practical possibilities and familiarity with means of exercising political pressure, legally or extra-legally, they themselves will cease to rely on mystical solutions, and the cargo myth will decline to the status of folklore. Naturally this process will be assisted by the present policy of the Australian administration of introducing representative local councils. Of course these will not remove all grounds for discontent, but the discontent will be expressed in demands for a fuller share in the political system.

In South Africa we can see the two possible developments that I have suggested following parallel streams in the Ethiopian churches and *Mission des Noirs* on the one hand, and the Zionist churches on the other. The former place their hope in a vague future; their rites assert their solidarity but are not conceived as means to bring about a direct result. The latter offer immediate results, but only on the personal plane. In the data given by Balandier we see how these two attitudes can be combined in what is ostensibly the same religion; the less sophisticated adherents, and those less exposed to indoctrination by the leaders, introduce into it the magical beliefs and extravagant hopes that might have given rise to independent religions had not a single organization made itself dominant in a wide region.

There are, of course, Christian sects which believe in the imminence of the millennium, and the best known of these, the Watchtower Movement, is at work in two of the three regions that I have discussed and very likely among American Indians as well. In comparison with local cults it, like the *Mission des Noirs*, has the prestige derived from the possession of its own doctrinal writings, which re-interpret the dominant religion in a manner favourable to the aspirations of the subject group. As a proselytizing body it has the immense technical advantage that it can produce literature on a large scale in a language understood over a large part of the world. We may guess that it will come to supersede the cults which appeal to local myths.

CONCLUSIONS

The similarities between events in such widely separated regions will not occasion any surprise to readers who are accustomed to recognize the same social processes at work wherever small-scale societies have been drawn into the orbit of industrial civilization. It has been remarked that the similarities in fantasy interpretation of the new situation would repay the attention of psychologists.

As regards the general characteristics of these movements, the Ghost Dance, with its complete rejection of the new world, stands in sharp contrast with the eagerness for participation in it represented by the cargo cults. I have suggested an explanation in the fact that the South Pacific peoples, whatever disturbing experiences they may have had in the early days of European contact, were not, as social groups, forcibly detached from their accustomed environment and whole way of life. Obviously those Indians who welcomed the Ghost Dance belief eventually accommodated themselves to their new circumstances as other tribes already had.

In the information from the South Pacific and from Africa we can see a development which corresponds to an increase in rational understanding of the situation. The naïve belief that the solution of material problems depends on control of supernatural

power can be seen giving way, in New Guinea, to an understanding of political forces which may still be naïve but is at least
more realistic. In Africa, where external trade gradually penetrated the continent through long centuries, there was no sudden
appearance of a wealth of material goods to be accounted for
only in terms of a miraculous source, and we know of no
parallels to the cargo cults. Here the fact of political subjection
itself is the theme of the independent religions, and they look for
their ideology not to traditional myths but to the Old Testament.
In the examples we have studied the millenary element plays a
relatively small part; the relegation of the idealized world to a
remote and indefinite future corresponds to an acceptance of
reality such as we find also in the final phases of the Ghost Dance.

It has been remarked that syncretic religions tend to flourish
in colonial territories where the direct expression of opinion on
political questions, and the formation of organizations for this
purpose, are not allowed. This is only a part of the story, however.

Sundkler's explanation of the South African churches is
conceived largely in these terms. He almost seems to invite us to
see them as coming into being to satisfy ambitions for which
there is no other outlet. One can, of course, understand the
desire of a subordinate in a mission church for a wider field of
authority, and recognize with him that it has led to many a
secession – but would *the same men* have founded political parties
if these had offered equal opportunities for leadership? One may
more readily assent to the proposition that religious *organizations*
will be formed in circumstances where other types of organization
are liable to be suppressed; their significance then is as much in
the expression of internal solidarity and differentiation from other
social groups as in the emotional appeal of their doctrine. But
the suggestion that there is a quota of some kind of energy
which will come out in religion if it cannot come out in politics
is almost like Williams' interpretation of the Vailala madness in
terms of the need for excitement. In this case it is relevant that
Christianity does make specific promises which colonial rule does
not implement. The discrepancies between its teaching and the
actual standard of governments which profess to uphold it have
led in Europe to the formulation of atheistic ideologies; in
Africa they lead more readily to the elaboration of rival theologies.
In those areas where Christianity has not been identified with a

dominant group, because there is no settler population belonging to that group, alternative religions have not gained importance. As it happens, political activity has latterly had freer rein in those territories, again because there is no settler population seeking to preserve its dominant position. But the need for a *religion* that corresponds to widely held aspirations is surely as important in the creation of the new sects as the need for a means of expression of some kind or other, or for an instrument for the activities of ambitious men; one can see this in the presence of millenary sects alongside the religions of hope deferred, and alongside such organizations as political parties and trade unions. Looking into the future of those territories where the dominant African group are the orthodox Christians and dissident sects are not prominent, one may ask whether one day new religions of the under-privileged will arise there too.

13

Clientship in East Africa[1]

The word clientship calls for some definition. In some societies it is a relationship involving very specific obligations, those of the client being more onerous than those of the patron. It can be described in this way in Ruanda, where more than one writer has interpreted it as a form of oppression. I would rather see it as a relationship of mutual advantage, though, since it is essentially one between unequal partners, the advantages are unequally distributed. I would also question the assumption that it is forced upon the client by the patron. If, as appears to have been the case in Ruanda, it was impossible for a member of the lower stratum to exist without the protection of a patron, this was *de facto*, not *de jure;* it was the result of the total political situation, and it seems to have been almost equally necessary for a good many members of the upper stratum to attach themselves to patrons. In other societies the making of a specific clientage relationship was a matter of choice, and it was often chosen by people who saw in it the way to social and political advancement.

Perhaps one might offer a minimum definition of clientship as 'a relationship of dependence formally entered into by an act of deliberate choice'.

It is my contention that such relationships are at the basis of the development of the kind of power which we associate with the office of chief, and, as the organization of government becomes more complex, with the type of political system that we call the state.

No doubt this proposition should involve me in a definition of the state. In his recent volume on the Acoli, Girling (1960) maintains that the distinction between states and stateless societies is meaningless, with the implication that every political system is a state. He further says that the Acoli have had states as far back

[1] Reprinted from *Cahiers d'Etudes Africaines*, **II**, no. 6, 1961.

as their history can be traced. On his showing it would be interesting to discuss whether the Acoli have or have not enough of the characteristics usually associated with the state to fall into this category. I think the distinction is still a useful one. For the purposes of my argument I still find useful as a description – not a definition – of a state type of political system that used by Fortes and Evans-Pritchard twenty years ago to characterize their 'Type A' societies. These, they said, were 'societies which have centralized authority, administrative machinery and judicial institutions . . . and in which cleavages of wealth, power and status correspond to the distribution of power and authority'.

This gives me a starting-point for my present argument, since it is my contention that clientship can develop in the presence of quite small inequalities of wealth, and that the loyalty of a client to his patron gives the latter the power, independent of entanglements with competing structural groups, which is essential to the appearance of an authority overriding all of these.

This can be seen at a very simple level. One example is the difference in the clan organization of the eastern and western areas of the Gusii country as described by Philip Mayer (1959). The western, lower-lying section is divided according to a classic pattern between six tribal territories. In each there is an 'owning' clan, on which immigrants have been grafted by classic processes of fictive adoption. Among the six western tribes the 'owning' lines claim no superiority in rank or power over the 'adopted' lines with whom they share their territory. Each is autonomous and seeks the mediation in disputes of its own elders.

In the seventh tribal area, Getutu, the original owning clan of Nyakundi has maintained itself as an entity distinct from later immigrants. These have not been 'naturalized' by any myth of adoption, and all must look to the authority of Nyakundi elders for the peaceful settlement of disputed claims. The reason for this, as Mayer interprets it, lies in the location of Getutu on high ground out of reach of Masai and Nandi raids. Refugees from the other tribes fled to Getutu and there attached themselves to leading men – that is elders of wealth above the average – offering services in return for protection. Women refugees were taken as wives and enabled the Nyakundi clan to multiply at a great rate. But the status of the men is more significant for the present argument. A single man would receive bridewealth cattle from his protector, and in virtue of this would be known as a 'bought person' (this did not imply slave status). 'Bought persons' could never establish an indefeasible claim to live in Getutu, though they were safe as long as they remained loyal to their protectors. They did not constitute a lower class in the sense that they were expected to treat all Nyakundi with deference. But they had a peculiar political function. When a Nyakundi elder sought to enforce the payment of a debt he sent a body of his 'bought persons' to collect from the recalcitrant debtor. Thus, if there was resistance which led to fighting , the fighting did not involve hostilities between the 'real sons' of Nyakundi, for whom the ideal was to live in amity. This ideal, be it noted, could not have been contemplated but for the presence of the 'bought persons'.

Another example of clientship in politics on a very small scale is that described by Jean Buxton among the Mandari (1958). Here again, the original client is a refugee, and, as Godfrey Lienhardt has pointed out, essentially a kinless man. Just as the picture of the Gusii refers to events of an era before the *pax Britannica*, so here, although one gathers that the Mandari envisage the possibility of new clients appearing at any moment, the observable fact is that certain persons are the clients of the petty chiefs because an ancestor became so on some occasion vaguely located in the past. Some are said to have been found wandering in the bush; in these stories the chief takes the initiative in offering his protection, an element which emphasizes the reciprocal advantages of the arrangement. There were formal ways of symbolizing the client's wish for protection and leaving the chief to take the first explicit step. Different reasons were given for the appearance of clients. Some were survivors of famines, epidemics or war; some had had to leave their own people because of a quarrel or had commited an offence; some had lost the contest for a headmanship.

Clients built their houses in a ring around that of their protector and so formed a defence against surprise attack. An individual client was obliged when called upon to go with his protector on a journey as bodyguard, porter and cook, to take messages for him, to wait on him at council meetings, to work on his fields. When there was fighting between the chiefdoms the clients were employed as spies, and today they are expected to report to the chief any evidence of disloyalty within his domain.

The client is not wholly dependent on his protector, nor is he expected to be continuously at the latter's disposal; he has his own fields and stock. Moreover, protection is not limited to permission to settle. The protector has the same obligations of vengeance, and of support before the courts, to a client as he has to his own kin. A favoured client can exercise a good deal of influence through his control of access to his master. The sanction for generous treatment is the desire of the chief to attract a following. It is regarded as entirely permissible for a client to transfer his allegiance. At the same time this could be regarded as a treacherous act, and in the past clients who were suspected of this intention were sometimes killed. This was the essential inferiority of the client's status; the chief would avenge him against outsiders, but there was nobody to avenge him against the chief. In the last analysis the diffuse sanctions of a reputation for fair dealing as a chief may have been a better protection for the client than anything he himself could do.

We know very much less of the status among the Shilluk (Evans-Pritchard 1948) of the 'Reth's people', who came to be regarded as one lineage despite the diversity of their origins. Their ancestors were war captives, homicides, or men who had been possessed by the spirit of Nyikang, the half-divine ancestor incarnate in every Shilluk king. Also some were just poor men who saw a better future in service to the Reth than in tilling their own fields. The last category at least illustrates the point that in some cases clientage may be a humble man's voluntary choice. The *bang Reth* lived around the royal palace. It was their duty to defend the Reth against the attacks of rivals, and it seems that sometimes, if a lineage engaged in a feud were intransigent in refusing to accept compensation, he could put pressure on them by mobilizing his people on the other side.

But, as I indicated earlier, it is among the Interlacustrine Bantu that clientage is most fully developed. Their rulers depended for the maintenance of their authority and extension of their power on subordinate chiefs who were bound to them not by kinship but by clientage, and who indeed were necessary to them for support against the rivalry of their lineage mates. Every ruler had his client chiefs, and these had their own clients.

It was only in the Tusi kingdoms of Ruanda and Urundi that a chain of clientage stretched from the ruler to the humblest peasant and apparently embraced the entire population. Even here, however, the relationship was initiated by an act of deliberate choice.

The peoples for whom we have information on this subject are the Ganda, Soga, Nyoro, Ankole and Ruanda (with a little supplementary detail about the Rundi). All these can be described as stratified societies in the sense that the total population can be divided broadly into two classes. For the Ganda and Soga the classes are 'chiefs' and 'peasants', and the essence of this distinction is between persons with the right to allocate land and persons who depend on them for land to cultivate. For the Ankole and Ruanda the classes are distinguished by names of ethnic significance (Hima and Iru in Ankole, Tusi and Hutu in Ruanda). These are divisions, in terms of traditions which are probably historically true, between conquerors and conquered; they also divide those who live by the possession of cattle from those who can at best acquire very limited rights in cattle. The Nyoro come in the middle; here the upper class no longer own cattle, and in fact their superiority now rests on their control of land, but they still think of themselves as an aristocracy of cattle people.

Patron-client relationships may link members of the upper and lower classes, or they may link members of the upper class; very rarely they may link members of the lower, as in Ruanda, where some Hutu had their own clients.

In the most superficial descriptive terms the obvious distinction between types of patron-client relationships turns on the question whether they are created by the transfer of cattle. This does in fact correspond to more significant differences in the nature of these societies and their problems. It is a truism that pastoral peoples are more warlike than agricultural ones, and this is sometimes interpreted as meaning that dependence on agriculture makes people pacific. It might be truer to say that it offers less incentive for warfare; the raiding of cattle is the easiest form of plunder in the world, and this to some extent explains the turbulence that seems to have characterized both Ankole and Ruanda in the recent past. Certainly it is clear that in the nineteenth century this region was the scene of intense competition in empire-building, in which the Ganda took as active a part as the pastoral peoples, and that the Ganda themselves were torn asunder by the 'religious wars'.

Nevertheless one does not get the impression that the protection against physical violence obtainable through clientage was as significant in Buganda as it seems to have been in Ankole and Ruanda.

In both these territories the relationship was created, as are so many social relationships among pastoral peoples, by the transfer of cattle. In Ankole the ruler, the Mugabe, alone had clients, and all his clients were Hima. They entered into this relationship by an act of homage which included a gift of cattle, but for any Hima other than the Mugabe to receive such homage was tantamount to a rejection of the Mugabe's authority, and was practicable only for people on the fringe of the territory which he controlled.

As Oberg (1940) reconstructs the picture, the client relationship was entered into voluntarily and could relapse or be renewed. It was initiated by an offer of service and a gift of cattle to the Mugabe. The offer of service involved, essentially, an undertaking to join in war expeditions when called on and to present to the Mugabe a share in the spoils of any raid organized as a private enterprise. The client was expected to repeat periodically the assurance of his loyalty expressed by a gift of cattle.

For him the advantage of the arrangement was his claim on the general protection of the military strength of Ankole against attacks from outside, and on immunity from revenge raids not authorized by a judgment of the Mugabe. If a client lost all his herd in a raid or an epidemic, he could expect the Mugabe to give him cattle to start a new one. He received his share of cattle captured in raids in which he fought as part of the Mugabe's forces.

In this description the entry into the client relationship seems to be synonymous with recognition of the Mugabe's political authority. If this is so it must have been in practice obligatory on all Hima living in territory that was indisputably his. One can hardly imagine a polity in which people who accepted the obligations implied in clientship were interspersed among others who did not. But one can readily imagine that on the periphery of his domain clients might disregard their obligations. Since this implied that they did not consider the Mugabe's protection worth having, such men must have contemplated either attaching themselves to a neighbouring ruler or building up an independent following of their own. But since there was some latitude in the obligations of a client – in assiduity in visiting the Mugabe and offering him gifts – there was room to distinguish between those who found it worth while to stand high in his favour and those who did not.

In comparing African political systems as we know them from ethnographic accounts, we are in the difficulty that we cannot know how far the contrasts that we see are matters of historic fact and how far of the selective interests of ethnographers and their informants. The contrast between the voluntary nature of clientship as described by Oberg among the Ankole and its obligatory nature as seen by Maquet in Ruanda is a case in point. In Ruanda, as seen by Maquet, the whole population were linked by patron-client ties, and this in spite of the fact that there were elaborate military and political administrations, high posts in which were, of course, allotted by the king to his own immediate clients. A difficulty in Maquet's account is the absence of detail on judicial processes, which are mentioned only enough to indicate that they existed.

As Oberg shows us Ankole, only persons appointed by the Mugabe as tax-collectors were entitled to make demands on the property of Iru peasants. In Ruanda it would appear that a Hutu had no rights at all to secure possession of property except in so far as these were guaranteed by his patron. In Ankole a Hima who killed an Iru was not required to pay compensation; in Ruanda it seems possible that a lord would avenge the killing of a Hutu client, as he certainly would that of a Tusi if called upon to do so.

From Maquet's description of Ruanda (1954) the essentials of the patron-client relationship were the same whether both parties were Tusi or one Tusi and one Hutu. The actual services demanded of a client must have varied to some extent with his status. If the great lords, clients of the king, were called upon for menial services, they doubtless sent their own clients to perform them. The humblest type of patron whom we can conceive would have only one client, a sort of general-purpose man.

As elsewhere, clientage is thought of as relationship freely entered into for the sake of the advantages which it is expected to bring. The stereotyped form of words from the would-be client to his chosen patron is: 'Give me milk; make me rich; be my father'. Here the client did not bring gifts, but the patron gave him one or more cows to herd – a way of creating a social bond that is common among East African cattle people. The client had the right to their bull calves, to their milk and that of their female offspring, and to their meat and hides when they died. It was also possible, apparently, for a Tusi client to secure clients for himself by placing in their care the offspring of the cows received from his lord. But none of these female animals became the property of the client.

While the link created by the transfer of cattle had both symbolic and material significance, the reciprocal obligations of lord and client were much wider than those involved in the custody of cattle. The client was liable for personal service when called upon – to attend on his lord on journeys, at war and when visiting the court. Clients were employed as messengers. Each client of a chief was responsible for maintaining a portion of the reed fence which surrounded his homestead. Hutu clients tilled their lords' fields. Some were made responsible for domestic duties such as cooking and brewing.

The lord on his side was expected to be a generous protector, to give his clients material help at need, to avenge a homicide if the client's lineage was not strong enough, to care for his widow and young children if they were left unprotected, to speak up for him if he was involved in a case in the king's court, and to pay any fine which he might incur there.

Although this relationship was initiated voluntarily, it usually became hereditary. Maquet does not mention any question of change in a client's position on the death of the lord, but he says that on the death of a client the lord could take back his cattle. Also he could apparently override the lineage choice of successor and himself appoint another member to the position. (This seems to be the clear meaning of Maquet's statement; i.e. it is not a matter simply of transferring the custody of the cattle to some other member of the lineage. It is possible that in some cases the client-ship cattle constituted the major part of the client's substance. But it would be interesting to know whether the 'designation of another heir' in fact implied that succession to lineage authority could depend on the wishes of the lord.)

Evidently the patron–client relationship linked descent groups as well as individuals, though at the same time it was possible for young men as they grew up to choose where they would offer their services. One man could be the client of many lords, and if necessary would send some other member of his family if called upon by more than one at the same time. In cases of divided clientship it seems clear that no one patron could intervene decisively in the choice of a successor.

This system created a series of links of personal dependence running right through the society. Under it, every individual, or at least every household head, had his place on some line of relationships of superiority and subordination created by the transfer of custody of cattle. Yet one cannot say that the status of client, or even that of lord, is an index of higher or lower rank in the society as a whole, since nearly all Tusi were simultaneously lords in some relationships and clients in others. Indeed the system has very little bearing on what has been classically regarded as the stratified structure of Ruanda society, namely the division into the cattle-owning Tusi and agricultural Hutu who could herd but could not own cattle, and the recognition throughout the society of the superiority of *all* Tusi to *all* Hutu.

In the predominantly agricultural societies, notably Ganda and Soga, clientship in the sense of a specific personal relationship embraced only that minority who chose to seek advancement by attaching themselves to persons in authority. Among these two peoples, and also in Bunyoro, the territorial subordinates of the hereditary rulers were personal followers appointed to their posts as a reward for services. The client relationship there was not a necessity of survival for the weaker members of society, as Maquet represents it, but the key to advancement in status. Paradoxically enough, however, it is in these societies that a relationship analogous to that of patron and client divides the whole population into upper and lower classes. This arises from the fact that territorial authorities traditionally had the right to allocate land, and that large numbers of persons preferred to apply to a chief for land rather than keep to land on which they had a claim by virtue of kinship. All persons living within the area of authority of a chief had the same obligations towards him, and all persons everywhere had to render these services to some chief; it would be as accurate to call them the political obligations imposed on all the population as to call them personal services to a particular individual. But the Ganda word for seeking land from a particular chief – and analogous words in neighbouring societies – does imply the making of a personal relationship of clientage.

And the traditional division of Ganda society into 'chiefs' and 'peasants' was in essence a division into those who had the right to allocate land and those who had to apply for it. This is why, at the time of the Uganda agreement, the chiefs were so appalled at Sir Harry Johnston's plan to disregard their rights over land; it would have obliterated the essential basis of the distinction between social classes. At that time they were not in a position to calculate the economic advantages that they were later to gain from the freehold ownership of land. It is interesting that, under an arrangement which seemed at first to have changed the whole basis of land holding, the relation of landlord to tenant is still conceived as one of political authority; the landlord is described by the same word as a political chief and the distinction between landlord and tenant is still fundamental in the stratification of Ganda society.

If, however, this relationship is to deserve the name of clientship it should perhaps be called passive clientage – I am *not* proposing that this should become current as part of standard terminology – and thus distinguished from the more active relationship of personal service through which people in these societies secured advancement in life. This relationship does not seem to have been initiated by any formal act. We read of ceremonial declarations of loyalty when a man was appointed to a chiefship, but this event comes nearer to the culmination of the relationship than to its inception. Moreover, it might not even be voluntarily initiated. I mean by this that the Kabaka and leading chiefs of Buganda had the right to claim as their servants boys and girls from the children of their subjects. It was also possible for a father to send a son to join the chief's retinue, thus securing favour for himself and a prospect of future advancement for the boy, from which his relatives might profit. The stories, like all such stories, tell how promising youths were recognized by their patent merits, promoted to more and more responsible service and eventually perhaps commended to the Kabaka. No doubt other factors helped to attract the chief's attention in one direction rather than another. Clientship in this case is the principal avenue of social mobility. It does seem to be the fact that in Buganda it was far more important than descent as a means of attaining high status, and also that the most important political positions were not claimed by particular descent groups.

In a comparison of Buganda with Ruanda from this point of view we see that in both cases the ruler had his subordinate authorities, appointed at his choice, whom we may reasonably call client-chiefs. In Buganda those who were given authority over large areas had their own subordinates chosen by themselves, who might even follow their patron if he was transferred to a different chiefship. Apart from this there was no system of what might be called 'private clientship'; only persons appointed by the Kabaka had the right to allocate land and the authority over peasants that went with this right, and all such authority was exercised in the last resort on behalf of the Kabaka. In Ruanda any man with cattle in excess of the needs of his own household could build up a client following. If we are to count all Ganda peasants as clients of chiefs, we can say that they have to become so because in a subsistence agricultural economy nobody can live without land to cultivate. But in Maquet's analysis the client must have a lord, not because he needs cattle, but because he needs protection.

I have suggested that one should expect greater turbulence among pastoral peoples, and this may be in itself a reason why Ruanda clients sought the protection of other men than the territorial representatives of the king. There are questions to be asked about the relationship between the king and lords with numerous clients. The Ruanda army system, which allocated the whole manpower of the country to specific fighting and herding units (without of course requiring them to be on active service all the time), must have provided a powerful obstacle to attempts to carve out independent principalities, though perhaps not to fighting as part of the contest for power between chiefs or lords. The small amount of data on Urundi so far published by Trouwborst (1959) has several references to fighting between chiefs, and indeed can be read as suggesting that support in fighting was a client's main duty, though one of his case-histories refers to chiefs who were deposed as a punishment for fighting, and another to a chief sent by the king to settle a dispute between two others. A man who had been a direct client of the king of Urundi recalled many wars against rebellious chiefs. There are of course also references to rebellions in the traditions of Ganda history. The consolidation of central authority and establishment of the 'King's Peace' in Western Europe is one of the most interesting of historical themes; but we shall never be able to trace its counterpart in the region of the Great Lakes.

Fallers' (1956) discussion of the position of client-chiefs in Busoga starts from the point that is also my starting-point: the need for any ruler, of however small a state, to be able to count on a following whose primary loyalty is to him and not to any one section of the society (in African conditions a lineage). He also shows, however, that in the small Soga kingdoms offices which were originally filled by clients chosen for their personal loyalty came to be regarded as the lineage property of their descendants. Nevertheless, these headmen's lineages recognize their origin in a client relationship; the claim to political authority in itself distinguished them from the field of equal competing vengeance groups.

Clientship, then, is a basis of social differentiation in two different ways. On the one hand, it creates formally recognised relationships of superiority and subordination, defined by other criteria than seniority. On the other, in some societies it is the main channel of social mobility. But the reason why I think it is interesting is that it seems to be impossible to build up predominant power at one point in a society unless the aspirant to power has a following of people who are more closely bound to him than they are to other members of the society. At the stage where the rewards of loyalty are small, such a following can only be built up from people who have nowhere else to turn – the kinless or those whose kin have rejected them. As power grows, the service of its holder becomes more attractive and the field of clientship expands.

14

Witchcraft as a Problem in the Study of Religion[1]

Witchcraft is popularly thought of as a subject for students of folklore. How are witches imagined, such students ask? Are they believed to fly through the air on broomsticks, or on some other means of transport? To have familiar spirits, and are these animals or something else? To act independently or in bands? How are they supposed to exercise their power, and how does one recognize a victim of it? Such matters of superficial description have been the subject of many books, and they appear to have a permanent fascination for the general public.

Most anthropologists working in Africa have found that the belief in witches is a fundamental part of the world-view of the peoples they have studied, and that it can properly be seen, not as a ridiculous superstition, but as a necessary part of their belief in the universe as a moral order. Such a belief is itself generally characteristic of peoples who have little knowledge of scientific causation, and who just because of this are unwilling to recognize the possibility of that accidental conjunction of causal factors that we call chance.

In a universe ordered in accordance with moral law, suffering – and in particular its most common form, sickness – should be deserved. An explanation of sickness is necessary so that the victim and his kin may take measures to remedy it, and for primitive peoples the explanation is commonly found in the displeasure of some non-human personalized being. The reaction of these beings is not thought to be arbitrary; if they punish, their anger must have been merited. Possibly the acts that incur their anger may not be such as would be strongly reprobated in western European society. An ancestor spirit may be angry because it has

[1] Reprinted from *Cahiers d'Etudes Africaines*, **IV**, no. 15, 1964.

not received its due in sacrifices; to some observers a reaction of this kind may seem to bring the objects of worship too close to the level of their human worshippers. Nevertheless, to be negligent in making offerings to the ancestors is to fail in an obligation. The principle generally accepted is that all suffering is deserved.

But in practice this is clearly not so. A sick man may examine his conscience and find that he is innocent. The general opinion of his neighbours may not agree with him in some cases; but there are always some cases where public opinion will hold that he has done nothing to merit punishment. Then there must be some agency which inflicts undeserved suffering. The explanation is found in the activity of the witch.

This is why I have suggested that beliefs in witchcraft are part of the corpus of beliefs that we commonly call religion. Some explanation of undeserved suffering is a necessary part of any conception of a spiritual world which supports the order of society.

The effect of this whole belief system, however, is to make every case of sickness, and sometimes of misfortune of other kinds, the occasion for discussion of the sufferer's behaviour and the respects in which he may have offended. Such a discussion is as important in asserting the socially accepted norms of conduct as is the public reaction to offences recognized as such. In most African societies the central point of the discussions is the consultation of a diviner, whose skill is believed impartially to identify the agency responsible for the sickness.

In many societies the witch is conceived as a person who in the nature of things cannot be identified. In such societies the witch is not believed to use material substances to attain his ends; therefore there can be no question of seeking evidence of his activities. He is thought to have the power of witchcraft born in him; sometimes this is believed to an actual physical substance, but one that could only be detected by an examination of his entrails after his death. Occasionally it is believed that the witchcraft substance operates without the witch's own volition.

In most societies people can describe the appearance of a witch as they imagine it, but often they believe that witches are adept at concealment, so that the person who looks least like a witch may actually be one. Thus an individual who is suspected has no valid defence. A belief system of this type is impervious to rational argument, and allows the person who thinks he is a victim of witchcraft to direct suspicion in whatever direction he chooses. The parallel with witch-hunts in western society is obvious.

In African society the accepted picture of the witch is the personification of the anti-social, and in this way also ideas about witches play their part in the system of social control. The witch is conceived as a person whom all dislike and whom none would wish to resemble. When children are overtly taught to avoid witches, and particularly not to provoke their anger, they are actually learning what kind of behaviour to avoid if they themselves wish to be regarded as good citizens and not suspected of witchcraft. Witches are thought of as ungenerous, unsociable persons, envying the good fortune of others – as persons who lust after meat and therefore may actually consume the flesh of their victims, or cause them to die in order that a funeral feast should be held, or both at once.

The formulation of the qualities of a witch is then partly a way of emphasizing the kind of behaviour that is socially approved. From another point of view it is a way of symbolizing the contrast between the social order and the 'savagery' that lies outside it. A witch as pictured by the Dinka of the southern Sudan is associated with those creatures and activities that are typical of the wild, uncultivated land, in opposition to the homestead, the symbol of the human community and its order. To the wild land belong animals and evil spirits, and the witch is assimilated to them. He is thought to do his work at night, the time when only evildoers are afoot. He is associated with night-birds and venomous animals, and in particular the black cobra, the most dangerous of all snakes. This snake is sometimes referred to obliquely as 'the thing of the wilds'. A witch is believed to attack his victims by smearing the blood of a cobra on objects in the homestead which they will touch. Finally he is believed to excrete in the homestead, thus, again, behaving like an animal, and defiling the mud floor which is always kept smooth and clean.

Among the Lugbara of the Uganda-Congo border the concept of witchcraft is associated with the concept of God as a being of dual aspect. God in the sky is the creator of social order. God in the earth is connected with darkness and the uncultivated bush, and witches are associated with him. Other peoples imagine witches as walking upside down – a very obvious symbol of reversal of the natural order.

But it is highly significant that the 'collective representation' of the witch is not evoked when a person thinks he is actually the victim of witchcraft. When this happens the victim and his friends do not ask whether a suspicious person corresponding to the ideal description has been seen around the homestead, or whether they have found cobra's blood on their cooking-pots. They ask who has a grudge against the sick man. Herein lies the greater social significance of the belief in witchcraft. Against whom are accusations of witchcraft directed?

Philip Mayer has offered as the essential feature of the witch that he is the traitor within the gates – a man from whom friend-ship should be expected but from whom instead comes injury. The victim does not suspect someone with whom he could be openly at enmity; he would pursue his quarrels with such a man in the chief's court, or even by directly assaulting him; the witch must be some member of the circle of neighbours and kin within which it is not decent to quarrel openly. As Mayer has put it, 'Witches and their accusers are individuals who ought to like each other, but in fact do not'.

Accusations of witchcraft are not made equally in all African societies. Among the Dinka, Lienhardt tells us, people may complain that they have been attacked by an unknown witch, but they rarely name a suspect, since to do so would be to arouse the anger of his kinsmen and friends.

In other societies, however, accusations of witchcraft are made openly. It is interesting that where this is so witchcraft is conceived as being in some sense an involuntary activity, or one in which the person accused is not thought to be wholly responsible. This is one aspect of the belief that the power of witchcraft is inborn. The Zande of the southern Sudan, where Evans-Pritchard made the first sociological study of witchcraft, express their view of it in this way: A man cannot help being a witch. He may be quite ignorant that he is a witch and quite innocent of acts of witchcraft. In this state of innocence he might do someone an injury unwit-tingly, but when he has on several occasions been exposed by the poison oracle, he becomes conscious of his powers, and begins to use them with deliberate malice. It is thus possible on some occasions for a man to be identified as a witch without his being the subject of moral condemnation.

One might almost say that undeserved sickness is ascribed to an irrational principle operating *through* human beings but without their volition. It is reported from Ghana that many people, particularly women, voluntarily accuse themselves of witchcraft; but simultaneously they exculpate themselves by the argument that their witchcraft power was given them, against their will, by some other person. The belief that a witch has a familiar spirit may partially exculpate the human agent held responsible for a sickness – or, more especially, a death. Thus among the Ndembu of Northern Rhodesia it is believed that it is the familiar spirit of the witch (a miniature creature in animal form) which actually kills the victim. But the spirit's activities are set in motion when its owner is angry; therefore, it is dangerous and wrong to give way to anger – another context in which the belief in witchcraft acts as a sanction for the norms of conduct.

One must distinguish between those accusations of witchcraft which are made between individuals in the heat of an altercation and those that are made in cold blood when a diviner has identified the witchcraft of some individual as the cause of a specific case of sickness. The former are probably made in all societies. There must be some connection between the uttering of threats to bewitch and the making of accusations, in the sense that where people threaten they must expect to be accused, but I do not know that any anthropologist has worked this out.

But the administration of the poison oracle, or any other method of divination to identify the witch, does not operate in a vacuum. The diviner is asked to use his skill to choose between certain possibilities, and the possibilities are those that have occurred to the victim of sickness, to his friends and possibly to his enemies (this is a point to which I shall return later on). In the case of the Zande the sick man, according to Evans-Pritchard, is angry at his sickness, and he places before the oracle the names of all the people he most dislikes, whom he believes to have wronged him in the past and who wish to harm him further.

In Zande country, however, the consequences of being identified as a witch are not serious. A person so accused is expected to express regret, to deny knowledge of his own witchcraft and to cancel its effects by the simple rite of blowing cold water from his mouth. Anyone so accused will go through these stereotyped actions, but many of them are privately indignant, deny the possibility that they are witches, and hint that the accuser has not really consulted the oracle at all.

The key point in Evans-Pritchard's discussion of this situation is that people ascribe the responsibility for their misfortunes to enemies who dare not harm them openly. He did not develop this theme so far as to ask the question in what kind of relationship this kind of hatred develops, but this has been a central question in many later studies.

It has been remarked that an accusation of witchcraft may be the means of bringing to a head a conflict of the kind that accepted norms do not permit; this is another way of putting the point that I quoted from Philip Mayer. It provides a reason for the secession of part of the population of a village, in face of the accepted ideal that members of a village should remain united and that division is the greatest misfortune. The greatest of evils, the presence of a witch, provides a valid reason for it. Thus accusations of witchcraft play their part in the rivalry between members of a lineage for control of their dependent kin, and so in the competition to build up a following that is chacteristic of traditional African society.

A people whose beliefs in witchcraft have been very fully described are the Nyakyusa of south-western Tanganyika, the subject of several volumes by Monica Wilson. Their conception of the witch might be said to be the classical African type: a witch is born with a snake in his entrails; thus he has an innate disposition to envy, hate and destroy his neighbours. If a body is opened up after death – as seems to have been regularly done in pre-colonial days – the snake, it is said, can be seen (in the form of some kind of swelling of the bowel no doubt). Witches lust after meat, and kill their neighbours in order to share the funeral feast: they also magically feast on the flesh of the living and cause them sickness. Also they drink the milk of cattle, causing them to go dry. They envy anyone who is unusually prosperous; and this belief may perhaps be called a social sanction in an egalitarian society.

Nyakyusa believe that it is the snake, flying through the air at night, that attacks people and cattle; and that there are certain other people who also have snakes inside them, though these are beneficent snakes. Such persons they call 'defenders'; they are able in dreams to see the attacks of witches approaching, and they send out their own snakes to fight them off. Any person may be a defender, but a part of the *rite de passage* which headmen go through before their installation is treatment with medicines to give them the power of defence against witches.

Among the Nyakyusa accusations of witchcraft do not seem to be made at critical moments of conflict. The conflict that ends in lineage fission is not endemic to their society, because residence is based on generation and not on descent, and because the social system provides for expansion in the division of the chiefdom into two in every generation.

An example of such conflict may be given from the Yao of Nyasaland, studied by Mitchell. The Yao believe that witches operate only against their own matrilineal kin – that is within the unit which ideally should be completely solidary. The mythology of witchcraft here asserts that witches kill their kinsmen in order to feast on their flesh along with their fellow-witches. For preference they kill those relatives whom they have reason to hate. This belief is a sanction for amicable relations between lineage mates.

But it can also be appealed to in justification of a breach of those relations. It is a commonplace of lineage organization that members of a lineage, though they may be solidary against outsiders, are often divided among themselves by rival claims. These may be claims to a share of lineage property or to autonomous control of one's recognized share. Or they may be claims to independent authority over a section of the lineage. The latter form of rivalry is characteristic of the matrilineal peoples of Nyasaland and Northern Rhodesia, and a number of British anthropologists have shown how the belief in witchcraft is used to justify the secession from the village of a section of the kin group. Such secession is deplorable by African standards. The unity of the village is the ideal, and it is the responsibility of its head, the senior man of the matrilineage, to care for its members in such a way that there will be peace and contentment among them. But it is every man's ambition to have his own village, in which he holds authority over his sisters and their children. For a younger brother this is not a permissible ambition; he should wait till he succeeds to authority when his elder brother dies. He cannot compete with the head of his own village; he can attain authority only by leading a secession. He may be able to attract a number of the villagers to himself because they do not like the headman, but this fact by itself would not justify a division of the village. The ultimate justification is given when sickness in the village is ascribed to the witchcraft of the headman.

A case recorded by Mitchell from the Yao illustrates this point. A woman and her two children fell sick. The village headman, the woman's elder brother, should, as their guardian, have consulted a diviner to find the cause. But he did not do so, and presently their mother, who was also living in the village, sent for a younger brother, who was living elsewhere with his wife's kin. This man asked the headman why he had done nothing about the sickness in his village. The headman replied that he was too busy working in his garden to go looking for diviners. The younger brother then offered to consult the diviner. The verdict of repeated divinations was that the headman was killing his sister and her sons by witchcraft. When the woman actually died, the younger brother announced that he was taking the lineage members away to a new village; and the original headman was left with only his own children and some lineage kin of his wife.

At various times in the course of these events, attempts were made to hold the village group together. But what finally made the division possible, at the same time as making it seem necessary, was an actual death, which was ascribed to witchcraft.

But accusations may be symptoms of social conflict and yet not have the cathartic effect of precipitating a final division. As Turner has described them among the Ndembu of Northern Rhodesia, they are made on the occasion of some natural disaster such as an epidemic of sickness, but they are directed in such a way as to express the rivalry of sections of a lineage for control of a village.

In the village where Turner did his ethnographic work, a division appeared to him to be inevitable, but the inhabitants themselves were not aware of this. They felt, rather, that the presence of witches among them was destroying amicable relations, and that these might be restored if a witch was identified and driven out; and eventually an old woman was expelled.

Why are old women so often suspected of witchcraft? For the Ndembu Turner answers that old women often have grievances against their own kin, who fail to maintain them adequately, and above all do not give them meat. In many African societies witches are believed to be greedy for meat, and Monica Wilson has remarked that this can be correlated with the intense interest in meat characteristic of people who eat it rarely. The Ndembu do not own cattle; their source of meat is hunting. There are strict rules about the distribution of the meat caught, and many of the most serious quarrels arise when these are broken. In such situations the claims of old women without close kin are not strong. So they may often be heard grumbling that no one gives them meat; moreover, they have no one to defend them by identifying someone else as the witch. Therefore an old woman is apt to be made the scapegoat when the village has been angered by a death.

Of particular interest are those peoples among whom the witch and the agent of deserved punishment are thought to derive their power from the same source. Such a people are the Lugbara of the Nile-Congo divide, who have been described by Middleton. They are an acephalous, patrilineal society, recognizing no authority other than that of the heads of kin groups, a type of authority that in the nature of things is supported by moral and ritual sanctions and not by force. Their religious system includes belief in the existence of a number of different supernatural agents of misfortune, and particularly of sickness. Unlike many African peoples, they do not believe that death itself can be attributed to the work of evil agents; for the Lugbara it is God who decides when a man is to die, and this decision is not in the nature of a punishment. (Perhaps it is worth mentioning here that those peoples who ascribe deaths to witchcraft do not always hold rigorously to this explanation; for example Turner records an occasion when an ambitious man, accused of bewitching the village headman in the hope of succeeding him, replied that there was no reason why he should do so, since old men die in the course of nature. And we learn of the Luhya of Kenya that at funerals it is the duty of one of the elders to prevent people quarrelling and accusing one another of witchcraft by reminding them that all men must die. Theories of witchcraft are not treated as objectively valid laws which hold good at all times; they are appealed to when they provide a way of pursuing human conflicts.)

Returning to the Lugbara, although they hold that God himself is responsible for death, they do not make him the centre of their religious cult. This is concerned with the ancestors, and it is to the ancestors that the Lugbara ascribe their existing social order. God created the world, but the ancestors prescribed the customs of the Lugbara. Shrines are built at which offerings are made to the ancestors collectively. But the more recent patrilineal ancestors, those whose names are known and their personalities remembered, have their individual shrines; and it is they who are thought to be directly interested in the behaviour of their living descendants, and to punish actions of a nature to destroy the unity of the kin group. The remoter ancestors may send sickness as a protest against the neglect of their shrines. 'We have waited many years,' a Lugbara quotes the ancestors as saying, 'our hunger conquers us, our child has not given us food.'

The more recent ancestors, however, are so close to the living that they can read their thoughts, and thus it is possible for a living man to call on them to punish an injury to himself. Only certain men can do this; in fact, it is possible only for heads of descent groups and particularly elders. By elder in this context is not meant any old man, but the particular old man who is recognized as the senior in a descent group of wide span, the man whose moral authority the members of the group should obey. He must be the senior living member of the group; as such he is closest to the head – 'he is near his father who told him the word of the ancestors'. Within such a descent group there are subdivisions, each with its own head; they too may invoke the ghosts of their immediate ancestors. But no man whose father is alive may be the custodian of a shrine, and no man who does not have a shrine can invoke the dead. The older a man is, the more effective his approach to the dead is believed to be.

The process which Middleton calls 'invocation' is not quite what the ordinary connotations of that world would suggest. It is not public; in fact no words are spoken, for it is believed that, if an elder were actually to utter his indignation in a spoken complaint to the dead, their reaction would be so fierce that the object of his anger would die. The actions that are held to justify an appeal to the dead are actions contrary to the norms of kinship; flouting the authority of an elder, striking a senior kinsman, quarrelling openly with a kinsman, stealing from him or deceiving him, failing in one's duties in the distribution of a dead man's property or the guardianship of his widows and children. All these kinds of act provoke indignation in right-minded persons, and the indignation of a man who is close to the dead can bring down their anger on the offender.

But the indignant elder does not display his indignation. He says nothing, but sits near the shrine thinking about the offence that has angered him. The dead become aware of his thoughts and punish the offender – as he intends they should. Although he does not speak, he does more than merely feel angry while he goes about his everyday affairs; he is deliberately concentrating on his anger in a way that should make the dead aware of it.

It is to be noted that there need be no publicity at any point in this procedure. Although a man may threaten to invoke the dead, it is only when someone is sick and a diviner consulted that the question arises whether his sickness was sent by the dead in response to an elder's anger. At this point the offended elder usually comes forward and says he did indeed invoke the dead. If his invocation proves vain, nobody need ever know that he made it. But there is so much sickness among the Lugbara in their cold mountain climate that this kind of failure is unlikely.

Now what is particularly interesting about the Lugbara is the way they describe the state of mind that leads people to invoke the dead. Their word for it is *ole*, and in the context of the kind of situation I have been describing this could reasonably be called righteous indignation. A sense of outrage is one of the equivalents that Middleton gives. But it is also used by the Lugbara for feelings of a much less elevated kind. They say, for example, that a man feels *ole* when another's dancing is admired while he is neglected; or when he sees another eating good food which he does not offer to share. This kind of sentiment would be more aptly called 'envy'; and here we find ourselves right in the field of motives attributed to a witch. Nor is this surprising, for in Lugbara opinion witches too are prompted by *ole;* and the word used for the process of setting the power of the dead in motion – *ole ro* – is the same that is used for the activity of witches.

A consequence of this way of looking at things is that for the Lugbara witches are not a distinct class of persons; the same individual may be regarded as an elder calling on the dead in support of the social order and a wicked man using occult power, and such conflicting interpretations are by no means unusual. (This again bears out the point that I made earlier, that there need be little relation in practice between the popular image of a witch and the characteristics of the individuals who are accused of witchcraft). For the Lugbara the crucial question is whether a man is, or is not, entitled to use a power, the nature of which is ultimately unexplained, to bring harm to others. Here, therefore, the direction of accusations must be closely correlated with the social structure. Typically they are brought against senior men claiming authority, by juniors who wish to repudiate this authority and establish their own autonomy; and Middleton has shown, as have Mitchell and Turner, how accusations flourish at a time when a descent group is about to split in two.

With the Lugbara, however, the accusation of witchcraft is not simply a justification for hostility between people who ought to be friends. For them authority is bound up with the claim to be able, and entitled, to invoke the dead in the interests of the social order; therefore a man who is seeking to assert himself as an elder, and one who has the backing of the dead, will openly claim the responsibility for sickness among his kin group, and this will be described as witchcraft only by those who dispute his claim to authority. In essence, for the Lugbara, the distinction between the elder invoking the dead and the witch is that the first is using occult power in the interests of the kin group, and the second in the pursuance of his own personal quarrels. But the question whether a man is a witch is itself decided by the question who is subject to his authority; if he is the head of his victim's descent group he *must* have been acting with justification. If he is an outsider to his victim's descent group – because they have established their autonomy under their own elder – he *must* be a witch. Old men – men who are getting too old to exercise their authority effectively – are most likely to be slighted by their juniors, or to consider themselves so; therefore, they have most occasion to appeal to occult powers, and their right to do so is most often disputed. Middleton has remarked that when Lugbara appeal to divination two conflicting theories of the cause of the sickness are usually put forward, one being that it has been caused by invocation, the other that it has been caused by witchcraft.

A further point can be illustrated from the beliefs of the Lugbara. Since in their eyes witchcraft is the illegitimate use of a power which is not of itself evil, they must have an idea of some other type of act which is in all circumstances evil. They find this in an activity which in most African societies is not thought to be unambiguously so. This is the use of material substances to cause harm by magical means. In most African societies it is thought that this may sometimes be done with justification – for example, as a means of redress against an unknown thief. But in the eyes of the Lugbara this is the activity that can never be justified; it is prompted by pure malice and strikes indiscriminately.

The Nyakyusa do not explain many cases of sickness by the anger of the ancestors. But they have an explanation that in some ways resembles the Lugbara invocation of the dead. It is that if someone flagrantly breaks a social norm, people will whisper comments on his action, and the actual wind of their voices – the 'breath of men' – will attack him with a chilling and eventually fatal sickness. Here we have in its clearest form the conceptual opposition between deserved and undeserved suffering and their different causes. But at the same time the effect of the 'breath of men' is linked in Nyakyusa thought with the power of witches. Sometimes the guardians of morality, the defenders, are believed to call on the witches to attack people who offend against the norms of society in various ways. One way is by failing in the obligation of sharing food, or in the duty to provide a feast when the occasion of a death or a marriage calls for it; one can see why the witches, with their greed for meat, could be called in to attack such a man. But other actions too may lead to this mystical punishment by public opinion; want of respect to elders, or from a wife to her husband, or any other manifestation of pride – of attempting to exalt oneself above one's station, to 'surpass' one's seniors as the Lugbara would put it.

The Nyakyusa do not resort immediately to divination to discover the source of sickness. The first measure to be taken is for the village headman to denounce the unknown witch. This is thought to be sometimes enough to make him desist from troubling his victim; but if the sick person does not recover, an accusation is made by one of the 'defenders' who are believed to see the witches in dreams. If the accused person is guilty, he ought to admit the charge; this is tantamount to repentance, and the effect of the admission should cancel the effect of the witchcraft. Naturally most people indignantly deny it, and in the old days they offered to undergo the ordeal of drinking *mwafi*, a medicine which an innocent person was supposed to vomit. A man who failed to prove his innocence was driven out of the village.

But here we come to another of the ambiguities in witchcraft beliefs. To have been convicted of witchcraft does not make a man an outcast. Not only will another village receive him, but after a little time his own village may ask him to come back. The neighbouring village, neutral in the case in which he has been condemned, accept him with the reasoning that they have nothing against him. His own fellow-villagers argue that one who has been shown to have the power of witchcraft is by that very fact well placed to be a defender of the village against other witches.

The two-faced image of the witch appears in even more striking form in Nadel's account of the Nupe of Northern Nigeria. Here it is believed that the most dangerous witches are always women, and that they are organized into a guild comparable to the human cult associations so common in West Africa. The members of this guild, of course, are unknown; when they are engaged in their evil work they make themselves invisible. But their leader *is* known; and she is in fact the head of the market women, the arbitrator in their quarrels. Or this was so in the remembered past. This woman is said to have been formally appointed by the chief of the town to restrain her fellow witches and prevent them from carrying their anti-social activities too far. When a witch was believed to have been active, it was for this woman to identify her and offer her up for punishment. This is perhaps the most striking example that we have of the identification of witch and defender.

But Nupe traditional organization also provided for a purpose that has come to be associated in other parts of Africa with the tension created by social change, and with the refusal of colonial rulers to countenance the traditional methods of identifying and dealing with witches. This purpose is the final cleansing of the community from the evil of witchcraft. This was the responsibility of an actual association with known membership. The initiates of this association were believed to have power over the ancestor spirits and to be able to make them appear; and they were able to mobilize the power of the ancestors not, as in some other societies, to punish ordinary evil-doers, but to punish the witches themselves. The head of this society was appointed by the king of Nupe himself. The cleansing ceremony consisted in a day-long dance by masked figures representing the spirits. All the women were gathered in the market-place, and from time to time a spirit-figure would bend over one of them, thereby identifying her as a witch; the witch might buy herself free, but otherwise she was killed in the bush.

A community which believed that it was afflicted by the activities of witches could appeal to the head of the association to hold a cleansing ceremony for it. But this man might himself propose to do this on his own initiative, of course with the approval of the king. The latter procedure came to be nothing more than a way for the members of the association to enrich themselves by the money that was offered to buy them off. It seems that in 1921 the whole economy of Nupe was upset by their exactions and it became impossible to collect taxes; after which their activities were forbidden. But although Nupe people realize that they were exploited by the assocation, they nevertheless say regretfully that they no longer have any protection against witches.

It is not surprising, then, that so many persons who claim to be able to get rid of witchcraft once and for all have appeared in Africa in recent years. Their activities have been described most fully in the matrilineal area of North-Eastern Rhodesia and Nyasaland, and notably by Audrey Richards and Marwick. Both writers have shown how the people integrate the messianic beliefs that they have learned from missionaries with their own conception of a world free from evil. Even if the purveyor of protective medicine himself disclaims miraculous experiences, it seems to be inevitable that they will be attributed to him; in particular he is usually believed to have risen from the dead. The technique of protection usually consists in offering medicine which both protects the innocent and destroys the guilty, in a sense a development of the ordeal motif. The 'prophet' or 'doctor' typically claims that his medicine, once drunk, will kill anyone who resorts to witchcraft at any time in the future.

The final elimination of witches is often among the promises made to their followers by the prophets of millenarian religions. This is not surprising if one accepts the interpretation of the belief in witches as a way of giving concrete form to the conception of evil. When in Africa these religions take on the form of a total reaction, as Balandier has so well described them, the theme of resistance to the colonial ruler becomes central and the fight against witches is temporarily forgotten. But since it is not really possible to achieve the golden age, the fight against witches is liable at any time to be renewed. It is, I think, of interest that some of the millenarian leaders have been closely associated with the detection of witches, or, if this has not been part of their original message, it has come to be ascribed to them by their followers. Balandier has noted that some of the followers of Simon Kimbangu claim that witches who seek to enter their church are detected by the fact that the baptismal water runs out of their hair. Millenarian prophets in other parts of the world have adjured their followers to desist from witchcraft. In both these attitudes one sees how the attempt to create the ideal world must involve the elimination of the principle of evil.

The proliferation of movements directed entirely to the elimination of witchcraft has characterized Central Africa for at least the last thirty years. Their success has usually been shortlived, because in the nature of things they cannot do what they promise. Some have attributed the enthusiasm with which they are received to the tensions created by the rapid social changes through which Africa is passing, others to the fact that the traditional recourse of accusation and punishment of witches is not countenanced by governments which do not believe in their existence. It would not be easy to demonstrate that the African of today more often supposes himself to be a victim of witchcraft than his grandfather did – although the South African anthropologist, Marwick, has said that witchcraft is suspected in all the new competitive relationships that this century has created, particularly where there is rivalry for the approval of a superior whose values are not fully understood, such as an employer or an agent of government. Certainly it has been recorded from Ghana that people who are dismissed from employment for drunkenness complain that witchcraft has made them drunkards. But perhaps the fundamental reason for the prevalence of new devices for the detection of witches is simply the human need to feel secure from ills against which there is no defence.

LIST OF WORKS CITED

Abbreviations: A.A.   American Anthropologist
                J.A.A.   Journal of African Administration
                J.R.A.I. Journal of the Royal Anthropological Institute

APTER, D. E., 1961. *The Political Kingdom in Uganda*, Princeton and London.

ASHTON, H., 1952. *The Basuto*, International African Institute, Oxford.

BAILEY, F. G., 1963. 'Politics and Society in Contemporary Orissa' in *Politics and Society in India* (C. H. Philips, ed.), London.

BALANDIER, G., 1955. *Sociologie Actuelle de l'Afrique Noire*, Paris.

BELSHAW, C. S., 1964. *Changing Melanesia*, Melbourne.

BERNDT, R. M., 1952. 'A Cargo Movement in the Eastern Central Highlands of New Guinea', *Oceania*, 22.

BOISSEVAIN, J. F., 1966. 'Patronage in Sicily', *Man*, N.S. 1, no. 1.

BROWN, G., and HUTT, B., 1935. *Anthropology in Action: An Experiment in the Iringa District of the Iringa Province, Tanganyika Territory*, London.

BURRIDGE, K. O. L., 1960. *Mambu: A Melanesian Millenium*, London.

BUXTON, J., 1958. 'The Mandari of the Southern Sudan' in *Tribes without Rulers* (J. Middleton and D. Tait, eds.), London.

CAMPBELL, J. K., 1964. *Honour, Family and Patronage*, Oxford.

CHINNERY, E. W. P., and HADDON, A. C., 1917. 'Five New Religious Cults in British New Guinea', *Hibbert Journal*, 15, pp. 230–40.

COHN, N., 1957. *The Pursuit of the Millenium*, London.

COLSON, E., 1950. 'Possible Repercussions of the Right to make Wills upon the Plateau Tonga', *J.A.A.*, 2.

COMMITTEE ON NATIVE LAND TENURE IN KIKUYU PROVINCE, *Report* of, 1933.

CRAWFORD, J. R., 1967. *Witchcraft and Sorcery in Rhodesia*, Oxford.

DE CLEENE, N., 1935. 'Les Chefs Indigènes au Mayombe', *Africa*, 8, no. 1.

EMMET, D., 1960. 'How far can structural studies take account of Individuals?', *J.R.A.I.*, 90.

EVANS-PRITCHARD, E. E., 1948. *The Divine Kingship of the Shilluk of the Nilotic Sudan*, Cambridge.

FALLERS, L. A., 1956. *Bantu Bureaucracy*, Cambridge.

FIRTH, R. W., 1936. *We, The Tikopia*, London.

—— 1938. *Human Types*, London.

—— 1951a. 'Some Social Aspects of the Colombo Plan', *Westminster Bank Review*, May 1951.

—— 1951b. *Elements of Social Organization*, London.

—— 1955. 'The Theory of "Cargo Cults": A Note on Tikopia', *Man*, 5, no. 142.

—— 1959. *Social Change in Tikopia*, London.

FORTES, M., 1945. *Dynamics of Clanship among the Tallensi*, Oxford.

FOSTER, G. MCC., 1962. *Traditional Cultures and the Impact of Technological Change*, New York.

GARBETT, G. K., 1960. *Growth and Change in a Shona Ward*, Salisbury.

GELFAND, M., 1967. *The African Witch*, Edinburgh and London.

GINSBERG, M., 1954. *The Diversity of Morals*, London.

GIRLING, F. K., 1960. *The Acholi of Uganda*, U.K. Colonial Office.

GUIART, J., 1952-3. 'The John Frum Movement in Tanna', *Oceania*, **22.**

HEYSE, TH., 1947. *Grandes Lignes du Régime des Terres du Congo Belge et du Ruanda-Urundi et leurs applications*, Brussels.

INTERNATIONAL INSTITUTE OF AFRICAN LANGUAGES AND CULTURES, 1932. 'A Five-Year Plan of Research', *Africa*, **5.**

KAMMA, F. C., 1954. *De Messiaanse Koreri-Bewegingen in het Biaks-Noemfoorse Cultuurgebied*, 's-Gravenhage.

KEESING, F. M., 1942. *The South Seas in the Modern World*, Institute of Pacific Relations, London.

LAWRENCE, P., 1954. 'Cargo Cults and Religious Beliefs among the Garia', *International Archives of Ethnography*, **47,** pp. 1-20.

—— 1964. *Road Belong Cargo*, Melbourne and Manchester.

LEACH, E. R., 1954. *Political Systems of Highland Burma*, London.

LEYS, N. M., 1924. *Kenya*, London.

LINTON, R., 1943. 'Nativistic Movements'. *A.A.*, **45,** pp. 230-40.

LOMBARD, J., 1967. *Autorités Traditionelles et Pouvoirs Européens en Afrique Noire*, Paris.

LOWIE, R. H., 1936. *Primitive Religion*, London.

MAIR, L. P., 1948. *Australia in New Guinea*, London.

MALENGREAU, G., 1947. 'De l'accession des indigènes à la propriété foncière individuelle', *Zaire*, pp. 235-70, 399-434.

MALINOWSKI, B., 1926. *Crime and Custom in Savage Society*, London.

MAQUET, J. J., 1954. *Le Système des relations sociales dans le Ruanda ancien*, Tervuren.

MARWICK, M. G., 1950. 'Another Modern Anti-witchcraft Movement in East Central Africa', *Africa*, **20,** pp. 100-112.

MAYER, P., 1959. *The Lineage Principle in Gusii Society*, International African Institute Memorandum XXIV.

—— 1961. *Townsmen or Tribesmen*, Cape Town.

MEAD, M., 1956. *New Lives for Old*, London.

MEEK, C. K., 1946. *Land Law and Custom in the Colonies*, London.

MILLS, M. E. ELTON, and WILSON, M., 1952. *Land Tenure*, Keiskammahoek Rural Survey, **4.**

MOONEY, J., 1896. 'The Ghost Dance Religion and the Sioux Outbreak of 1890' in *Fourteenth Annual Report of the Bureau of Ethnology to the Smithsonian Institute*, 1892-93 (J. B. Powell, ed.).

MORGENTHAU, R. S., 1964. *Political Parties in French Speaking West Africa*, Oxford.

MÜHLMANN, W. E., et al., 1961. *Chiliasmus und Nativismus*, Berlin.

MUKWAYA, A. B., 1953. *Land Tenure in Buganda*, East African Institute of Social Research.

NADEL, S. F., 1942. *A Black Byzantium*, London.
—— 1945. 'Land Tenure on the Eritrean Plateau', *Africa*, **15.**
—— 1947. *The Nuba*, Oxford.
—— 1951. *The Foundations of Social Anthropology*, London.
—— 1953. *Anthropology and Modern Life*, Canberra.
NASH, P., 1955. 'The Place of Religious Revivalism in the Formation of the Intercultural Community on Klamath Reservation' in *Social Anthropology of the North American Tribes* (F. Eggan, ed.), Chicago.
OBERG, K., 1940. 'The Kingdom of Ankole in Uganda' in *African Political Systems* (M. Fortes and E. E. Evans-Pritchard, eds.), Oxford.
PAUL, B. D., and MILLER, W. B. (eds.), 1955. *Health, Culture and Community*, New York.
PHILLIPS, A., 1945. *Report on Native Tribunals in Kenya*, Government Printer, Nairobi.
RADCLIFFE-BROWN, A. R., 1952. *Structure and Function in Primitive Society*, London.
REDFIELD, R., 1953. *The Primitive World and its Transformations*, Ithaca.
RICHARDS, A. I., 1935. 'A Modern Movement of Witchfinders', *Africa*, **8,** pp. 448–61.
SALISBURY, R. F., 1964. 'Despotism and Australian Administration in the New Guinea Highlands', *A.A.*, **66.**
SCHWARTZ, T., 1962. 'The Paliau Movement in the Admiralty Islands, 1946–1954', *Anthropological Papers of the American Museum of Natural History*, **49,** part 2, New York.
SMITH, M. G., 1960. *Government in Zazzau*, London.
SMITH-BOWEN, E., 1954. *Return to Laughter*, London.
SPICER, E. H., 1952. *Human Problems in Technological Change*, New York.
STANNER, W. E. H., 1953. *The South Seas in Transition*, Sydney.
SUNDKLER, B. G. M., 1948. *Bantu Prophets in South Africa*, London.
TROUWBORST, A. A., 1959. 'La mobilité de l'individu en fonction de l'organisation politique de Burundi', *Zaire*, **13,** pp. 787–800.
VELSEN, J. van, 1964. *The Politics of Kinship*, Manchester.
WARD, B. E., 1956. 'Some Observations on Religious Cults in Ashanti', *Africa*, **26,** pp. 47–60.
WELBOURN, F., 1961. *East African Rebels*, London.
WILLIAMS, F. E., 1923. 'The Vailala Madness and the Destruction of Native Ceremonies in the Gulf Division', *Papua Anthropological Reports, No. 4.*
—— 1928. *Orokaiva Magic*, Oxford.
WILSON, G., 1940. 'Anthropology as a Public Service', *Africa*, **13.**
—— 1945. *The Analysis of Social Change*, Cambridge.
WORSLEY, P. M., 1957. *The Trumpet Shall Sound: A Study of 'Cargo' Cults in Melanesia*, London.

LONDON SCHOOL OF ECONOMICS
MONOGRAPHS ON SOCIAL ANTHROPOLOGY

Titles marked with an asterisk are now out of print. Those marked with a dagger have been reprinted in paperback editions and are only available in this form.

1, 2. RAYMOND FIRTH
The Works of the Gods in Tikopia, 2 vols., 1940. (2nd Edition in 1 vol., 1967.)

3. E. R. LEACH
Social and Economic Organization of the Rowanduz Kurds, 1940. (Available from University Microfilms Ltd.)

*4. E. E. EVANS-PRITCHARD
The Political System of the Anuak of the Anglo-Egyptian Sudan, 1940. (New edition in preparation.)

5. DARYLL FORDE
Marriage and the Family among the Yakö in South-Eastern Nigeria, 1941. (Available from University Microfilms Ltd.)

*6. M. M. GREEN
Land Tenure of an Ibo Village in South-Eastern Nigeria, 1941.

7. ROSEMARY FIRTH
Housekeeping among Malay Peasants, 1943. Second edition, 1966.

*8. A. M. AMMAR
A Demographic Study of an Egyptian Province (Sharquiya) 1943.

*9. I. SCHAPERA
Tribal Legislation among the Tswana of the Bechuanaland Protectorate, 1943. (Revised edition in preparation.)

*10. W. H. BECKETT
Akokoaso: A Survey of a Gold Coast Village, 1944.

11. I. SCHAPERA
The Ethnic Composition of Tswana Tribes, 1952.

*12. JU-K'ANG T'IEN
The Chinese of Sarawak: A Study of Social Structure, 1953. (New edition revised and with an Introduction by Barbara Ward in preparation.)

*13. GUTORM GJESSING
Changing Lapps, 1954.

14. ALAN J. A. ELLIOTT
Chinese Spirit-Medium Cults in Singapore, 1955.

*15. RAYMOND FIRTH
Two Studies of Kinship in London, 1956.

16. LUCY MAIR
Studies in Applied Anthropology, 1957.

†17. J. M. GULLICK
Indigenous Political Systems of Western Malaya, 1958.

†18. MAURICE FREEDMAN
Lineage Organization in Southeastern China, 1958.

†19. FREDRIK BARTH
Political Leadership among Swat Pathans, 1959.

*20. L. H. PALMIER
Social Status and Power in Java, 1960. (Paperback edition in preparation.)
†21. JUDITH DJAMOUR
Malay Kinship and Marriage in Singapore, 1959.
†22. E. R. LEACH
Rethinking Anthropology, 1961.
23. S. M. SALIM
Marsh Dwellers of the Euphrates Delta, 1962.
†24. S. VAN DER SPRENKEL
Legal Institutions in Manchu China, 1962.
25. CHANDRA JAYAWARDENA
Conflict and Solidarity in a Guianese Plantation, 1963.
26. H. IAN HOGBIN
Kinship and Marriage in a New Guinea Village, 1963.
27. JOAN METGE
A New Maori Migration: Rural and Urban Relations in Northern New Zealand,
1964.
28. RAYMOND FIRTH
Essays on Social Organization and Values, 1964.
29. M. G. SWIFT
Malay Peasant Society in Jelebu, 1965.
30. JEREMY BOISSEVAIN
Saints and Fireworks: Religion and Politics in Rural Malta, 1965.
31. JUDITH DJAMOUR
The Muslim Matrimonial Court in Singapore, 1966.
32. CHIE NAKANE
Kinship and Economic Organization in Rural Japan, 1967.
33. MAURICE FREEDMAN
Chinese Lineage and Society: Fukien and Kwantung, 1966.
34. W. H. R. RIVERS
Kinship and Social Organization, reprinted with commentaries by David
Schneider and Raymond Firth, 1968.
35. ROBIN FOX
The Keresan Bridge: A Problem in Pueblo Ethnology, 1967.
36. MARSHALL MURPHREE
Christianity and the Shona, 1969.
37. G. K. NUKUNYA
Kinship and Marriage among the Anlo Ewe, 1969.
38. LUCY MAIR
Anthropology and Social Change, 1969.
39. SANDRA WALLMAN
Take Out Hunger: Two Case Studies of Rural Development in Basutoland, 1969.
40. MEYER FORTES
Time and Social Structure and Other Essays, in press.
41. J. D. FREEMAN
Report on the Iban, in press.